Heb 10: having the
roenie into the
Jesus, buy A new
has consecrated
That is to say, his flesh.

John and Mary Anthony
19645 Golden Rock Circle
Groveland, CA 95321

Heard . Heb 5:7

The Power and Promise
of Christian Prayer

Dale Van Steenis
with Greg Smith

Black Lake Press
TELL YOUR STORY
BLACKLAKEPRESS.COM

P 80 leadership in prayer meetings

Cover design by Greg Smith of Black Lake Studio.

Published by Black Lake Press of Holland, Michigan.
Black Lake Press is a division of Black Lake Studio, LLC.
Direct inquiries to Black Lake Press at *www.blacklakepress.com*.

ISBN 978-0-9824446-2-7

contact the author directly through his website:
www.leadershipstrategies.org

Acknowledgements

There are people who pray and then there are people who *pray*. It is the later group that has put a prayer print on my life. While this book is full of stories of great prayers from many places whose tales encouraged me along the way, it is the people below who touched me first and sustain me now.

First, from a formational and foundational point there were my parents, William and Lillian Van Steenis. They were faithful people to God and church and ministry and servanthood. Most importantly they prayed. Dad went to prayer meeting every Saturday night as faithfully as the sun rises and sets. He would also be found a full hour *before* most services with his face buried in an old wooden chair weeping in intercession. I will never forget seeing him in that position. Mom was an intercessor of the first order. Either alone or with a few other like minded ladies, she would petition heaven for hours. Many times I arrived home at odd hours from traveling and heard mother praying for various needs. That sound is with me still.

Second, my boyhood pastor, Bond Bowman, was, above all else, a praying pastor. Many times through the years I was in our church building and heard him pray. He prayed with desperation as though the people and needs he was praying about were matters of life and death. Perhaps, in reality, they were. On one occasion I passed a closed door behind which he was in prayer. I did not know a grown man could weep and sob at the level I experienced that day. His prayers were gripping, groan filled, laborious and *effective*.

Finally, my precious wife Gloria also carries a spirit of prayer. It is in her and on her.

She spends many hours a week in our home in prayer. The success of our children and the fruit of our ministry are directly linked to her availability to take God's burden and pray it into reality. Where ever ministry has taken me, I know it has been under girded from home through the praying heart of my dear wife. Thanks Gloria, for being who you are in Christ, and who you are to me.

Foreword

I received my call to preach at age 14. God called me with an audible voice and called me by my first name, John. It was an undeniable call. Soon thereafter my pastor came to my mother and asked her if he could take me into his care and teach me how to pray. I thought, "I'm not called to pray, I'm called to preach." That wise pastor knew a secret that must be eventually learned by those called into ministry as well as the laity, and that secret is this, "you'll never be successful in any kind of ministry until it is soaked in prayer. Prayer is your success. It is transforming."

Dale Van Steenis has been my personal friend for many years. I have always known him to be a man of prayer and a man that flows in the gifts of the Holy Spirit.

I had Dale come to minister while our church was still under construction in 1990. He was outside looking over the construction site and saw prophetically that honey was dripping from the unfinished structure. Dale proceeded to reveal to me that God was about to do a very powerful work through Brownsville. As a matter of fact, just months before Revival broke out in 1995, he called and encouraged me with a powerful prophetic word that revealed how to structure what God was about to send to our church and city. I've never forgotten those two encounters that impacted me in such a positive way. My subsequent relationship with Dale has been one that I have drawn strength from. He has a reservoir of life that I draw from and it flows from his prayer life.

When Dale sent me the manuscript on "Heard," I read it in one sitting. It is indeed a prayer manual because it takes us step by step through all the pitfalls we all encounter as we pray and seek God. I found myself encouraged, strengthened' and challenged.

I heard someone say long ago
sometimes prayer is like digging holes,
sometimes prayer is like planting poles,
sometimes prayer is like stretching wire,
sometimes prayer is like making contact.

Contact is what we live for. Don't give up until you connect and receive your petition from on high. Prayer indeed will transform your world.

John A Kilpatrick
Former pastor, Brownsville Assembly of God
Current pastor, Church of His Presence
Daphne, Alabama

Introduction

Some folks at church have helped me a lot. Those who helped me substantially are those who prayed long and often. I call them "moist" or "damp" pray-ers since tears usually accompanied their petitioning. Observing those persons, sometimes called intercessors, has deeply and permanently affected my life. The pages following bring some of them before you. May your life be impacted by their experiences. I believe the whole world is held together by those who pray and is an estimably better place because of them.

What has prayer accomplished anyway? We do not know precisely because we neither see nor know all the works of God (See Hebrews 11:32-40). One thing is certain: intercessors have made and are making a difference in our world through their prayers.

I am particularly interested in the lives of those who have prayed for many years with perseverance and passion. I am inspired by how they cling to God with dogged determination, often facing the demons of discouragement, resistance, and eroding faith. The spirit of these hardy warriors is summarized in the words of Karl Barth who once said, "To fold one's hands in prayer is the beginning of an uprising against the disorder of the world."

In my many years of world wide travel I have noticed, with alarm, a trend related to prayer.

Even in the largest church buildings there are only either very small rooms or public spaces designated for prayer. There appears to be a severe "lightening up" in terms of prayer efforts and prayer priorities. Recently, I picked up a monthly church calendar on which were posted eighteen prayer opportunities for the month. Wow, I finally found a church that is "doing the prayer thing." When I asked the prayer leader about attendance, I was told, "I am often alone and on the best of times, there are 3-4 people with me." That pitiful situation exists in a church with 6,000 in Sunday attendance. That church may be big, but it is also weak. Who calls on God these days? Do we still need him?

The Western church is blighted by a prayer famine. It is plagued with dry eyes, few tears, and no fire in the gut. There is little Elijah-like prayer with weeping and white-hot fervor. As a result, altars are vacant, congregants come in and go out the same, and the local culture remains unchanged. May I ask where the God of power is? There are many substitutes for the real Acts-level, God inspired, Holy Spirit-directed Church. Instead we get carefully crafted music presentations, non-offensive and non-challenging preaching, sparse, if any, time spent waiting for the Holy Spirit to work—well, you know those churches. But where can God be seen in his power and glory? How can we get to *that* environment? We are on the way to his best when we pray.

Hopefully this book will give its readers a "second wind" in prayer. God still answers. He said he would. So, I have included stories from near and far and from many contexts of life. Some prayers were made from absolute desperation. Others were a little less intense emotionally but important nonetheless. We live in a time when many voices speak out about how to do things, when many ministries claim "keys" to success. My encouragement is to pray again.

Chapter 1
Why Wouldn't We Pray?

We are used to hearing sales pitches. We are told that we should buy *this* product. Why? Well, because of all of its features and benefits. We should see *this* movie, try *this* restaurant, visit *this* church, go on *this* diet or read this book. Why? Well, here's a list of compelling reasons.

The assumption is that we need to be persuaded to act. Our default position is that we don't do anything unless we are presented with cogent and compelling arguments.

And so it's tempting to start a book about prayer by listing all the reasons that we ought to pray. I'm tempted to start by trying to sell you on the value of prayer, persuading you with a mixture of guilt and promises. That is, of course, how we convince each other to engage in other aspects of the Christian life, like tithing, charity or evangelism. I'm tempted to point out that God demands it, that it's our Christian duty, or that it's evidence of the sincerity of our faith. I could follow up the guilt trip by trying to sell you on all the positive benefits of prayer: you'll grow spiritually, God will bless you, the Kingdom will advance.

I could try and sell you, but I won't. Instead, I'd like

to start with a simple question: why *wouldn't* we pray?

I can understand why our default position is to not buy a new product, visit a new restaurant or read a new book without hearing persuasive reasons. Those things requires us to spend money or time that could be spent otherwise, and so we need good reasons to make that investment.

But prayer is different. If we are followers of Jesus, then prayer is as much a basic part of our existence as eating, drinking or sleeping. We might need to be convinced to try a particular food or drink, or to sleep in a particular place, but we don't need to be persuaded to eat, drink or sleep. Our default position is that we must do these things, that we will do these things. The questions are only about where, what, when and how.

Why should it be otherwise with prayer? As Christ-followers, do we need to be persuaded to pray at all? We can and should talk about methods and and strategies, but we shouldn't need to sell God's people on the idea that they ought to pray to him.

And yet the reality is that we do need to be convinced. For a variety of reasons many Christians don't pray very much, if at all. This is hard to comprehend. If we actually believe that through the resurrection of Jesus and the gift of the Holy Spirit we have the ear of our Father, then why don't we pray? If we really believe that we are, as the Church, the temple of his Spirit and his Kingdom is among us, then why don't we pray? If we really believe that we do not live by bread alone, but by every word that proceeds from the mouth of God, then why don't we pray? If we really believe that he will give us whatever we ask in his name, then why don't we pray?

Some Christians could articulate reasons why they shouldn't give money, or go to church, or share the gospel with their neighbor. They might not be good reasons—more like excuses—but they could articulate them nonetheless. But could any Christian give any reasons why they shouldn't pray?

In any discussion of prayer, this is the point where most contemporary Christians blame our lack of prayer on the modern world. It would be easy to say that it is the result of a depraved culture, weak leadership in the church, or the saturation of ungodly media. It would be comforting to believe that this is a new problem, and that back in the "Good Old Days" Christians wore their kneecaps out before the Father.

But that wouldn't be true. Even a cursory examination of the Bible reveals that God's people have always tended to neglect prayer, long before the curses of our modern world. Adam and Eve hide from God after disobeying him (more about that later). The Israelites have a pattern of choosing ceremony and sacrifice over prayer. The disciples cannot stay awake to pray with Jesus in the garden of Gethsemene. The letters of the apostles to the early churches exhort them to prayer precisely because they needed to be exhorted. Church history gives further evidence that our neglect of prayer is not just a modern phenomenon: Christian leaders are forever having to remind their flocks to pray.

For reasons that are hard to understand, God's people tend to neglect their most basic need. In fact, it makes more sense to discuss why we don't pray, rather than why we should.

If we think about it, it's not surprising that some Christians avoid prayer. People engage in self-neglectful,or even self-destructive behavior all the time. Some drink or take drugs that they know are harmful to them. Some don't get enough sleep, or drive too fast, or drive too fast when they're sleepy. They acknowledge that their behavior is stupid and dangerous, but they do it anyway. Some people never clean their house and live in disorganization or even filth when they know better. Some people don't balance their checkbook even though they know that they keep getting overdrawn. Some don't eat healthy foods, or get enough sleep, or drink enough water. When confronted, they admit that they know they ought to do those things, but they still don't do them. Some neglect their children or their marriage, even though they admit that their family is falling apart.

There are many reasons why people neglect their basic needs, or even destroy their lives. Why do Christians, who know better (or ought to), neglect their most basic need to engage in fellowship and conversation with God?

The first explanation is perhaps the simplest: they don't really believe in prayer. As Christians we *say* that prayer is the basic fellowship of a creature with its Creator, and that through Christ's resurrection and the gift of the Spirit we have access to the throne of grace, but perhaps some of us don't really believe it. It's one thing to acknowledge something intellectually, and another to believe it enough to act on it.

We have generally accepted intellectual knowledge

that is disconnected from our personal experience. For example, we all "know" that E=MC2, or that the gravity on Mars is 60% that of Earth, or that Mount Everest is 29,029 feet or that the human cell has 16 pairs of chromosomes because experts have told us so. I don't really understand how E=MC2, I've never been to Mars or the top of Everest, and I can't see my own genes. In the same way, theologians, pastors, and Christian writers tell me that I can enter the throne room of grace through prayer, and that if I delight myself in the Lord he will give me the desires of my heart. I "know" that because I believe and trust them. But if I've never *experienced* meeting God in prayer it's hard for me to believe that it's necessary or beneficial. I'm not compelled to act.

Sometimes we avoid prayer because we are avoiding God. It's absurd, of course, because we can never actually hide from him. But that doesn't stop us from trying. In the second chapter of Genesis, Adam and Eve are placed into the Garden of Eden. They apparently have an open and regular fellowship with God. They are naked, with nothing to hide. And yet, in chapter three we read about one of the most tragically comic moments in human history. They eat from the Tree of the Knowledge of Good and Evil, breaking the only rule they have been given. They immediately experience guilt, fear and shame. At that moment, they hear God coming. Apparently, he would walk in the Garden during the cool of the day and speak with Adam and Eve. As the Creator of the universe–the very One who spoke the stars into being and formed mankind from the dust–comes down the garden path they hide in the shrubbery, hoping that he won't notice them. Perhaps they hope that God, not seeing them, will forget about them and go away.

Sometimes we don't pray because, like Adam and Eve, we are hiding from God. Guilt, shame and or, fear drive us away from him. We avoid God because of what he might say to us or what he might *not* say. Of course this is silly: we can't hide from God. It reminds me of a friend who had a big, black Labrador retriever. When it snowed, the dog loved to play in the yard, and one of it's favorite "games" was to hide in the snow: it would bury its head in the snow, with its big black body poking out. It operated on a faulty premise: it thought that if it couldn't see my friend, then my friend must not be able to see it. In the same way, avoiding God in prayer does not make us invisible to him.

Some of us fall into a variation of this. We pray, but we do all the talking. Our prayers become a tiresome one-way conversation, not because we are relentlessly petitioning him, but because are are trying not to let him get a word in edgewise. We don't want to hear what we fear he will say.

Sometimes we don't pray because of simple laziness. Prayer is a spiritual discipline, it takes effort. That's hard to do in a world with so many distractions. We live with so much more *noise* than earlier generations in history. We are surrounded by televisions, radios, phones, computers, speakers blaring announcements, and signs flashing in front of us. If we are already not inclined to pray, we have endless other things to capture our attention. Prayer requires us to turn all that off or to get away from it. It takes effort to create the peace and quiet where we can make the effort to pray. That's a lot of work.

Some people give up on prayer because they are angry about unmet expectations. They have been hurt, and feel that God hasn't listened to their pleas or complaints. Perhaps at a particularly difficult moment in life they poured their heart out, hoping that God would respond in some way. When he didn't, they gave up on prayer. They believe in God, even trust in Christ for their salvation, but they feel like there is no point in asking God for things. They don't believe that prayer "works."

Some people don't know how to pray. At first glance, that seems incredible: after all, how difficult can it be to talk to God? Actually, though, many people avoid initiating conversations with other people: what should they talk about? How do they get around to the topics that interest them? How should they express themselves? Let's face it: sometimes prayer can feel like an awkward or weird one-way conversation, especially for the less-experienced. For many people, it does not come naturally. Many of us simply were never taught how to pray. Human conversation is an art, and conversation with God is no different. The simple, spontaneous, and heart-felt prayer is wonderful, but serious prayer is something that we learn to do. Hopefully, we learn by doing. But for those of us who have never had good examples or mentors, much less training, it can be intimidating.

When asking why Christians don't pray when they have no good reason not to we cannot discount the issue of spiritual warfare. Put simply, our enemy Satan does not want us to pray. He uses any means available, including manipulating the impulses above, to discourage us. He reminds us of our guilt and reminds us of times when God didn't respond to our prayers the way we expected him to. He tries to distract us and encourages us to indulge our laziness. Paul reminds us that, "Our struggle is not against flesh and blood, but against the rulers, against the authorities, against the powers of this dark world and against the spiritual forces of evil in the heavenly realms" (Ephesians 6:12). On the other hand, we must be careful that we don't make him out to be more powerful than he is. Paul goes on to say that with the shield of faith we can extinguish all the flaming arrows of the evil one, and that while, "the weapons we fight with are not the weapons of the world...they have divine power to demolish strongholds." (2 Corinthians 10:4).

We should also not blame the devil for our own sins of commission or omission. In the end, it is the weakness of our own flesh, our own sinful nature, which causes us to sin, even though we know better. As Paul says in Romans 7, "what I do is not the good I want to do; no, the evil I do not want to do—this I keep on doing" (Romans 7:19).

Regardless of the reasons why we don't pray, the bottom line is that many Christians are not so much neglecting a duty, but a basic need of their existence. The more sleep-deprived an insomniac becomes, the more frayed and ragged he becomes. The fewer calories an anorexic takes in, the weaker and less able she is to care for herself. A thirsty person who neglects to drink on on a hot day becomes ever-more dangerously dehydrated and susceptible to delusions. They aren't so much disobedient as foolish, nor are they really missing out on benefits as much as they are depriving themselves of life itself.

Like all our basic needs, prayer takes time and effort. We spend an enormous amount of our lives gathering food and drink, and consuming it. We spend perhaps a third of our lives asleep. There is always something we could be doing instead of praying. But the more we pray, and the

Prayer is a basic Need of our Existence

more experienced and effective we become at it, the less it feels like effort and the more it weaves itself into the fabric our existence. A mature human life, the kind of life God designed us for and longs for us to live, has eating, drinking, sleeping, loving and praying as its basic rhythms.

Mother Teresa was a Catholic nun who, for decades, ran a hospital for the poorest and sickest in Calcutta, India. Her ministry was an inspiration to millions, maybe even billions. In the 1980's, Mother Teresa was interviewed by television reporter Dan Rather. The following part of the interview clearly puzzled Rather, but was a remarkable insight into her spiritual life.

Dan Rather: "Mother Theresa, when you pray what do you say to God?"

Mother Theresa: "I do not say anything, I listen"

Dan Rather: "Well as you listen to God, what does he say to you?"

Mother Theresa: "He doesn't say anything, he listens."

Sometimes she and God just sat, listening to each other. Prayer had become an integral part of her life, like eating and drinking and sleeping. Her conversation with God had become like the slow and lingering conversations that stop and start between an elderly couple sitting on their porch. How odd would it be to live with someone for decades, and not speak with them? How odd would it be for two people who had spent all those years together, with all the intimacies of daily life, to have to verbalize everything? Eventually, couples like that learn to read

Basic Rhythms of Life

→ And take Time & Effort like
Eating — Drinking — sleeping — loving — praying

each other's body language, to interpret each other's sighs and silences, to anticipate each other's thoughts. It would be strange to ask *why* should they communicate with each other, when they couldn't help but to do so.

Why should we pray? A better question is: *why wouldn't we?*

Chapter Two
It's What We Do

All religions involve prayer. Muslims are instructed to pray five times a day, facing the city of Mecca. At the time of Christ, the ceremonial prayers of the Romans to their pagan gods were like elaborate incantations. Tibetan Buddhists hang "prayer flags" (little strips of brightly colored cloth) in the mountains to bring blessings from their gods.

While people of all religions "pray," it is what they imagine prayer to be that's different. For the Christian, prayer is fundamentally *a relationship with God*. It is not just offering praise, or confessing sin, or giving thanks, or bringing requests. All of those things are what we do *within* Christian prayer, but they aren't what prayer *is*. Nor are they ultimately the point of it. God doesn't want his people to pray because he needs to hear them say nice things about him. God doesn't need to be told what they did wrong (he already knows), or what they think that they want or need (he knows better than they do). God longs for people to be in intimate relationship with him. He longs for them to weave him into their lives.

I have a friend whose daughter recently graduated and moved away to another city. In the years before she left, their relationship was strained. The girl thought that she knew it all, that her dad wasn't "cool" and couldn't possibly understand her problems. A few months later, he got a phone call. She had a problem, needed advice, and called her dad. She wasn't asking for money, or to be rescued from a dilemma. She really wanted his input on a decision she had to make. The girl probably hung up the phone, went about her day and thought nothing more of it. But it was a profound life-moment for my friend. The problem they discussed was minor and easily solved, but that only made it more meaningful to him because it meant that she wanted to talk with him about the mundane details of her life. She invited him into her world.

Christian prayer is like that. God longs for us to invite him into our lives. Truthfully, we can't keep him out because he supplies our daily bread and counts the hairs on our heads (Matthew 10:30). But he longs for us to welcome him into our hearts. Like a father who doesn't want to get calls from his college kids only when they need money, he doesn't want us to pray only when we're in trouble. Nor does he want only a merely formal relationship, being invited to only our weddings and graduations. He wants to be a part of our daily routine and the mundane details of our existence. Christian prayer is the ongoing conversation of an intimate family.

This kind of prayer is so much a part of the Christian faith that, it's fair to say, it is simply what Christians do. Of course we worship, minister to each other, share the Gospel with the lost and try to help the orphan and the widow. But the most basic thing that Christians do is to try to live in intimate relationship with Christ with the help of the Holy Spirit. All those other aspects of the Christian life flow from us being children in ongoing dialogue with our Father (1 John 3:1).

The Gospel is the story of how this relationship got broken and was restored. We all remember the Parable of the Prodigal Son. A man had two sons. The younger one got tired of living under his father's roof and longed for independence. So he asked his father to give him his future inheritance early and set off to explore the world. It went well for a while, until the money ran out and his new friends abandoned him. He found himself starving in a distant land. He was desperate enough to take a job with pagans, tending their unclean pigs and eating the leftovers from the trough. Eventually, he came to his senses, remembered the abundance of his father's house, and decided to return to ask his dad for a job so that he wouldn't starve. Meanwhile, the father had been standing on the porch every day, scanning the horizon, waiting for his son to come home. When he saw him coming down the road, while he was still a long way off, the father ran out to the son and embraced him. His pig-stained clothing was replaced and he was restored into the family as a son. This is the heart of the Gospel: our Father longs to welcome us back into the intimate fellowship of the family. He has made that possible through the cross and empty tomb. He waits for us to come to our senses so that he can sit us down at the family table to join in the ongoing, daily conversation that is prayer.

God keeps trying to teach us this, trying to get us to come to our senses in this distant land. We find, in the history of God's people, four formative experiences in which they were supposed to learn to weave conversation with him into the fabric of their lives. In all of these God was trying to teach them that intimate relationship in prayer is simply what his people do.

The first of these formative experiences was in the beginning: intimate fellowship with God is what we did in Eden before the fall into sin. Adam and Eve were naked in the garden: no sin, nothing to be ashamed of, nothing to hide. We read in Genesis 3 that the Lord used to walk in the garden during the cool of the day. There was nothing preventing their intimate fellowship with him. It was how mankind was meant to live.

After they sinned they felt shame, which led to one of the most tragically comic moments in the Bible. Adam and Eve heard the Lord coming on his daily walk, and they hid in the bushes. Perhaps they were "shushing" each other, trying to be very quiet in the hopes that the Lord would go away. Did they really think that the Lord wouldn't know they were there, and wouldn't know what they had done?

Adam and Eve demonstrate what has shipwrecked the prayer lives of countless numbers of their descendants: shame and guilt lead to avoidance. It's not that some of us can't talk with God, nor that it's especially difficult. It is, after all, what we were made to do. But we don't want to talk to him because we don't want to discuss uncomfortable topics. Some of us know that the conversation will eventually get around to some of God's thoughts which we don't want to hear. So we hide from him, stay quiet, and hope that he'll go away. Intimate relationship with God is what we did in the garden, but that came to an end. Once outside the garden, prayer began to require sacrifice.

The second formative experience for God's people was their journey through the wilderness with Moses. Again, the point was to teach them to weave God into the fabric of their daily lives.

Moses, a fugitive from Egypt, was tending sheep on Mount Sinai. The Lord appeared in a burning bush and told Moses to go and fetch his people (who were slaves in Egypt) and bring them back to him. Moses, anticipating a potential problem, asked the Lord for his name. He imagined telling the Hebrews that "God" had sent him, and for the Hebrews to respond by asking: *"Which god? Who is this 'God?' Does he have a name?"*

And thus began a most unusual season in the history of God's people, as they got to know the Lord (whose name, "I am who I am," is rendered in our English Bibles as *Yahweh* or *Jehovah*). He took them out of Egypt and brought them to Sinai. He allowed Moses to bring seventy of the elders of Israel halfway up the mountain, where they had a picnic with him (Exodus 24:9-10). He allowed Moses to see the backside of his glory as he passed by (Exodus 34:6). Moses spent weeks up on the mountain with the Lord, receiving the laws which would govern every aspect of the Israelites' daily lives: worship, food, marriage, business, construction, hygiene, law, and so much more. For forty years they lived with the Lord in their camp, literally. Their tents were arranged around the tabernacle, where his presence dwelt. They ate, slept, bathed, married and had children in front of the Lord. He fed them with manna and quail. At times he appeared as a pillar of smoke or fire, and when he moved, they packed up camp and followed. This formative season in the history of God's people was meant to teach them—and us—to live in his presence, in intimate fellowship. Prayer is simply what God's people do.

The apostles lived in this way with Jesus for three years, which was the third formative experience meant to teach God's people that prayer is supposed to be part of the normal rhythm of life. God incarnated himself in the person of Jesus, and his principal disciples—the apostles—had the ultimate personal and intimate relationship with him. They ate meals with him, they slept beside him, they talked with him throughout the day about both profound and mundane things. They talked with him when they were tired, when they were excited, when they were frightened, when they were curious. Jesus and his disciples started campfires together, bought lunch together, argued together, even went to the bathroom together.

For the better part of three years Jesus became as much a part of their lives as their parents, siblings, or coworkers. In fact, in the Gospels it seems that conversation with him is so easy that they sometimes say things that pop into their heads without thinking. They express ambition, jealousy, worry and exuberance. They are their real selves with him.

This is what Christians do, or what Jesus was trying to teach us that we should do. He is not a politician or celebrity whom we aspire to know and in front of whom we pretend to be better than we really are. He is our master, our rabbi, our friend. We are to be our true selves with him, sharing with him the stuff of our daily lives.

Intimate fellowship in prayer is what it means to be his follower.

The fourth formative experience was the early Church. It's not a coincidence that it began in prayer. We read in the second chapter of Acts that the disciples were all together in one place (a room or a house) in Jerusalem when the Holy Spirit came upon them. They began to speak in other tongues as the Spirit enabled them. From that point on, the early Church was characterized by intimate prayer. The Holy Spirit gave direction, insight, encouragement and admonishment. In the Book of Acts we read about problems, even conflict, in the early Church. But we also get a picture of a Church that is animated by and open to the Spirit. The apostles, companions of Jesus, brought that experience into their leadership, and we see little of the formality and distance from God that characterizes Christianity at other times and places.

In their letters to the early Church, the apostles share their vision and desire for the Christians to open their lives to intimate relationship with the Lord. Peter says that Christ's followers are like living stones, being stacked together to form a temple with their lives to house the Holy Spirit (1 Peter 2:5). In Romans 8:26 Paul tells us that we should pray, even when we don't know what to pray for, because the Holy Spirit will intercede with groans that words can't express. That is the kind of intimate fellowship, the kind of ongoing (often non-verbal) conversation that God wants to have with his Church. It's what we do, or are supposed to do.

HEARD

There is another experience for God's people described in the Bible, but it isn't formative, because it hasn't happened yet. We read that in heaven, God dwells with his people, and conversation with him becomes a normal way of life. The communion and fellowship of Eden is restored. It is as if God were walking in the cool of the garden again, and there was no sin, no shame, no hiding.

This future intimacy in prayer isn't formative, it's *transformative* because it is a vision and a promise that pulls us forward. It reminds us that fellowship with God is not just what we *should* do, nor only what we *did* do, nor merely what we *do*, but what we *will* do. Seen this way, prayer is not just the means to cope with a broken world, it's preparation for eternity, a foretaste of what is to come. It is the prize for which we are being called heavenward, but more about that in the next chapter.

Chapter Three
For the Prize

We pray because of where it takes us, and because of who we become through it. Let me explain with an illustration.

Imagine a giant, upside-down cone. Its narrow end touches the ground, and it expands as it goes upward, out of sight, into infinity.

Imagine that you are standing in the bottom of its narrow end. It's cramped, and you don't have much room to move around. It is also completely dark.

Imagine that there is a ceiling just over your head, with a round door in it, like a manhole cover. You can reach up and feel around the edges.

Imagine that there is something you desperately want right through that opening. Maybe it's a job, or the ability to pay the mortgage next month. Maybe it's health for yourself or a loved one. Maybe it's faith for your son, or a Christian husband for your daughter. Maybe it's your plane landing safely, or the neighbor you've been inviting to church showing up next week. Imagine anything that you want strongly enough to pray for it.

Imagine that as you pray for that thing, you feel the

energy to climb up through the opening and scramble into the next level. It's not easy because the opening is tight, gravity is tugging at you and you're intimidated by the thought of what might be up there. But the more you pray, the more strength and courage the Holy Spirit gives you, and you pull yourself through. When you get there, you stand up, look around and realize three things.

First, God has answered your prayer. That thing that you wanted up here has somehow been resolved with God. Maybe not exactly in the way that you expected or even asked for it to be resolved, but you have peace and assurance that God has solved the problem in the best way possible. You are satisfied.

Second, you're now in a bigger space than you were in the level below. There's more room to move around. Also, the walls of the cone are just a tiny bit more translucent, and just a tiny bit of light comes through them. You can almost see the outline of your hand if you hold it up in front of you.

Third, you realize that something *else* you want is just above you, through another round opening in the ceiling over your head. Since prayer worked last time, you decide to pray again.

The same thing happens. As you pray, you feel the Holy Spirit give you the strength and energy to climb up through the hole into the next level. Again, the space is bigger as you go higher up and deeper into the cone. The walls are just a tiny bit more translucent, and there's just a bit more light here. When you get here, you realize that God has dealt with the thing that prompted you to pray your way to this level. You feel peace and confidence, knowing that he is in control of that situation. In fact, you feel a little silly that you were so nervous about it when you were down on the level below: had you forgotten how he took care of your previous need?

There's someone else on this level. You hear a voice, and in the dim light you shuffle over and find another Christian. They tell you that they also had some need and that praying about it enabled them to climb up here. As the two of you talk, you discover that you have some mutual concern, something that both of you need or want, and that it is probably overhead, through the opening in the ceiling above. Based on your previous experiences, you agree to pray for it together. The Holy Spirit gives you the energy and courage to climb upward into the unknown.

Again, you come into a wider, brighter place. Again, God assures you that he has dealt with the thing you were concerned about with wisdom and mercy. On this level there are several other people, with stories like yours. Again, you discover some mutual need or concern. Again, you pray together. Again, the Holy Spirit enables all of you to climb up and into the cone of his power and grace.

The higher up and deeper into God's Kingdom we go, the bigger and brighter it gets. As we begin our journey, we are compelled by needs and wants: hunger, illness, fear, worry, desire. These things prompt us to pray. When we pray, the Holy Spirit leads us upward and inward into the heart of God's presence and power. Our prayers are answered—often in unexpected ways—and we have greater confidence and peace in his sovereign grace. We can see more clearly, and as we realize that his Kingdom is bigger than we had known, we feel less confined. In fact, there are a few passages in the Old

Testament where the original Hebrew uses the image of a wide place, or an open space, to describe the freedom that God gives his people when he hears their prayer. The New King James Version translates the metaphor almost literally when it renders Psalm 37:7-8 as, "I will be glad and rejoice in Your mercy...You have set my feet in a wide place," and Psalm 118:5 as, "I called on the LORD in distress; The LORD answered me and set me in a broad place."

Along the way to these wider, open spaces we meet other Christ-followers, who are also moving higher up and deeper into the Kingdom of God. As we feel less stifled and alone, and as we see prayers answered and gain a peace that passes understanding, our concerns get bigger as well—not bigger in the sense of more desperate or despairing, but more about the Kingdom and less about ourselves. We begin to pray with others and for others. We begin to pray for things that we can see more clearly in these brighter, wider spaces. We pray with more confidence and as we do the Holy Spirit leads us higher up and deeper in. As we go, we are being cheered on by those who have gone further ahead: "Therefore, since we are surrounded by such a great cloud of witnesses, let us throw off everything that hinders and the sin that so easily entangles, and let us run with perseverance the race marked out for us" (Hebrews 12:1). Hebrews 12:22-23 goes on to tell us that on our journey we have "come to Mount Zion, to the heavenly Jerusalem, the city of the living God. [We] have come to thousands upon thousands of angels in joyful assembly, to the church of the firstborn, whose names are written in heaven."

Prayer drives us higher up and deeper into the

Kingdom of God. But let's be clear: prayer isn't magic. Our prayers are not incantations, means to manipulate the universe or heavenly forces. It is the Holy Spirit who leads us, enables us, refreshes us, encourages us, strengthens us, advocates on our behalf, and speaks for us when we lack the words. But prayer is the mechanism for the Spirit to move us up and into the Kingdom, because prayer focuses our longings and makes us attentive to the Spirit's work. As time goes on, we remember how God has answered our prayers by taking us to bigger and brighter places, cheered on by a great cloud of witnesses. We begin to enjoy the journey for its own sake. Seeing evidence of God's sovereignty makes us more confident in him, and we become less concerned with our wants and needs because we know that he will satisfy them all. We long to go higher up and deeper in. We pray, with others, to know him more. Prayer becomes not just a means to get what we want, but a motive in its own right: we love to pray not because of what we get, but because of what we experience through it.

Early in the Christian life, prayer gets us out of tight, dark places. As we mature in the Christian life, prayer takes us closer to "the prize." The term "prize" is used four times in the New Testament, all by the Apostle Paul. In 1 Corinthians 9 he points out that only one runner in a race wins *the prize* and encourages us to run our races like we are trying to be that one. A few verses later (9:27) he tells us that he trains his body and spirit like an athlete so that he will not fail to win *the prize* that he has preached to others about. In Philippians 3:14 he says that he is pressing on to win *the prize* for which God has called him heavenward (higher up and deeper in) through Christ. In Colossians 2:18 he warns against false teachers who would lead believers astray, disqualifying them for *the prize.*

What is "the prize?" It seems unlikely that it is merely salvation. The word Paul uses in Greek is *"brabeion,"* which was the award given to the victor in athletic games in the Greco-Roman world. The clear context is that it is something we strive to achieve, even to earn. *"Brabeion"* would be a weirdly inappropriate metaphor for our salvation, which is a free gift through the death and resurrection of Jesus. Christ strove for and won that prize on our behalf.

Paul must be talking about one of two things: he is either suggesting that through striving for heaven we prove that our faith is real, and not just an intellectual exercise, or he is describing our rewards in heaven, not entrance into heaven itself.

Our faith might be a gift, but how do we know that we have real faith? Jesus tells us that a tree is known by its fruit (Matthew 7:18-20). Not everyone who *talks about* Jesus *knows* Jesus. Not everyone who intellectually agrees with Christianity or goes to church on Sunday really has saving faith or has received the Holy Spirit. Paul tells us in Philippians 2:12 to continue to "work out our salvation in fear and trembling." I take that to mean that we strive, not to earn salvation, but to prove that it has really been earned for us. In other words, we work not to become saved, but to show that we are. So when we pray, and advance in the Kingdom, are we securing our prize by showing that our faith is genuine?

Or is "the prize" our heavenly reward? Jesus mentions heavenly rewards for our faith and works nine times in the Sermon on the Mount alone. There are hints throughout the New Testament that, for the saved believer, there are *degrees* of reward in heaven. Some serve Christ with more sincerity and fruit in their Christian life and taste that fruit in the next life: they win the *"brabeion."* Their prize is greater than those who did less with the gifts and opportunities God entrusted to them. If that is so, then what might their "prize" be? More jewels in their crown? A more luxurious cloud or bigger wings? A better spot in the heavenly choir?

I suspect that the prize is this: within this lifetime (and perhaps the next), some Christians climb higher and deeper into God's Kingdom than others. They move into wider and brighter spaces, full of more of the saints, than some of us. God's glory is more obvious to them because they can see it more clearly. They have greater confidence in his sovereign love because they have experienced, time and again, him responding to their prayer by revealing his grace and power. They have a peace that transcends understanding because, through prayer and petition in all things, they have brought their requests to God (Philippians 4:6-7).

Pagans may believe in magical incantations, but Christians believe in prayer. The right combination of words, or the right method of reciting them, does not grant our wishes. The Father's will is done by the Son, and we experience that through the Holy Spirit. Prayer focuses our longings and opens us to the work of the Spirit, who uses it to lead us higher up, deeper in, and closer to, the prize. The reward of a mature prayer life is to pray less for your own needs, because you have seen God meet them so often that you have complete trust in him. The reward of a mature prayer life is to pray in greater concert with the great cloud of witnesses who cheer on God's unfolding Kingdom. The reward of a mature prayer life is to walk in the freedom of wide, open places bathed in eternal light. The reward of a mature prayer life is to begin experiencing heaven in this life, so that the transition to the next is seamless.

Why do we pray? We pray because of where it takes us and who we become through it. We pray to earn the prize.

Chapter Four
Ask, Seek, Knock

*"It is God's memorial that in every generation
he hears prayer."*
– Reverend William Plummer

*"Now hear my prayers, oh listen to my cry. For my life is
full of troubles, and death draws near."*
– Psalms 88:3 (LB)

The two most extensive of Jesus' monologues in the New Testament are found in Matthew chapters 5 through 7, and John: 13-17. Both contain much teaching about prayer (secret, humble, and quiet), fasting and prayer, patterns of prayer, and how to request help from the Father. A relationship with the Father was one method Jesus taught to secure answers to prayer. John 16:23 says, "If you ask the Father for anything, He will give it to you in My name." John 15:7 promises, "If you abide in Me, and My words abide in you, ask whatever you wish, and it shall be done for you."

On the human side of the prayer equation, we are called upon to do two things. First, God insists that our hearts be turned to him, and second, that we ask, or make requests. We read in Hebrews 5:7 that Jesus made prayers with "loud crying and tears" and he "was heard." In Philippians 4:5-6, Paul encourages petitioning the Father. Unfortunately, there is a clerical division in the English translation that makes no sense at all. The last part of verse 5 is clearly part of verse 6. It reads as follows:

> "The Lord is near (verse 5b). Be anxious for nothing, but in everything by prayer and supplication [asking] with thanksgiving let your requests be made known to God (verse 6)."

Paul explains the means (the Lord) and the mode (petition) made in a spirit of thanksgiving—as the path to getting prayers answered. Asking is encouraged and permitted when clothed in a thankful spirit.

Asking Prayer

Asking prayer constitutes more than ninety percent of all praying. We have needs, and we ask God for help. This type of prayer is centered in things that touch us personally. Hence, asking prayer does tend to become self centered. It is me-related praying. All believers have this right in prayer and are encouraged to ask. However, to become a mature pray-er, one must grow in intercession, engage in spiritual warfare, pray for laborers to be sent, and for the peace of Jerusalem, etc.

We must also ultimately learn to pray "Thy will be done." 1 John tells us: "Beloved, if our hearts do not condemn us, we have confidence before God; and whatever we ask we receive from him, because we keep his commandments and do the things that are pleasing in his sight" (1 John 3:21-22).

These, then, are the conditions for receiving prayer answers from God. John 9:31 says, "Now we know that God heareth not sinners: but if man be a worshipper of God, and doeth his will, him he heareth" (KJV). God places importance on many things and *obedience is above them all.*

God does not answer petitions that seek nothing more than to satisfy self-indulgent passions and personal aggrandizement. By obeying his word, repenting of sin, and behaving properly, our minds and spirits are much more sensitive in weighing those things that we ask of him. But before we offer our petition, we should remember these words from Ecclesiastes 5:2, "Do not be hasty in word or impulsive in thought to bring up a matter in the presence of God. For God is in heaven and you are on earth; therefore let your words be few." In other words, any petitions sent to God ought to be well considered before they are made and, in all cases, stripped of excess words.

The tone of this verse is solemn. It is an exhortation to serious contemplation prior to bringing a request before God. If we place Ecclesiastes 5:2 side by side with what we learned from Romans 8:28, we can see that we need God's help, both in shaping our needs and requests and also in presenting them to him.

In the average prayer meeting, a considerable amount of time is spent asking for help for matters that, if answered, would make life a little more comfortable but which are relatively trivial when measured in the light of eternity. One measuring device to determine the quality of our requests is to ask the question: Is the Glory of God being served and/or seen in the request, or is it something to enhance my comfort zone?

Prayer that changes people and nations is of a deeper kind. Thankfully there are people who pray beyond their needs and consider God's will before anything else. God is near to this holy remnant that holds the world and its people together by their prayers and intercession.

Jeremiah 33:3 says, "Call to Me, and I will answer you, and I will tell you great and mighty things, which you do not know." The same prophet said, "You will seek Me and you will find Me, when you search for Me with all your heart, and I will be found by you, declares the Lord" (Jeremiah 29:13-14).

Seeking prayer

Asking prayer looks for answers to specific requests. Seeking prayer searches primarily for insight, for information, or revelation. It searches for those facts that will answer a life-related dilemma, to discover that which will bring a resolution or release. King David framed it this way:

"Hear, O Lord, when I cry with my voice,

And be gracious unto me,

When Thou didst say, 'Seek my face,'

My heart said to Thee, 'Thy face, O Lord, I shall seek.'" – (Psalms 27:8 KJV)

Obedient, patient seeking of the Lord will bring any honest seeker to a place of encounter with God. He reveals Himself to the persistent seeker. (See Jeremiah 29:13-14 above). His promise is, "I will be found."

2 Chronicles 7:14 is one of the most often quoted references to prayer in the Bible. This promise was given to Solomon on the night that concluded the dedication of the Temple, ending the single greatest week in the history of Israel to that point. God chose the quiet moments at the end of that dedicatory week to deliver a strong and important message to Solomon. The presence of God had been so strong it became visible and the priests could not minister because God had drawn so close. God then spoke to Solomon and told him that he, God himself, had accepted the temple as his own and placed his name there. Knowing the people's tendency to backslide, he uttered the following words on the last night of the dedicatory week:

> *"And if my people who are called by my name humble themselves and pray, and seek My face and turn from their wicked ways, then I will hear from heaven, will forgive their sin, and will heal their land."* – (2 Chronicles 7:14)

Integrity of heart, persistent seeking, and timing are all requirements for our prayers to be answered. God adds another when he says, "Seek my face." I believe that means to go on a dogged, relentless pursuit of God. Manifest hunger. Look for him. Appear before him with an attitude that says you will not be easily sent away.

Psalms 14:2 says, "The Lord has looked down from heaven upon the sons of men, to see if there is any who understand, who seek after God." Paul, speaking of the

Jews and Gentiles of his day said, "There is none who understands, there is none who seeks for God." (Romans 3:11). What a rebuke! We must be exactly the opposite and manifest hunger. Other verses say:

"Draw nigh to God and He will draw nigh to you."
– (James 4:8)

"Seek first the kingdom of God." – (Matthew 6:33)

"Call to me and I will answer you."
– (Jeremiah 33:3).

"Seek the Lord while He may be found."
– (Isaiah 55:6).

"He is a rewarder of those who seek him."
– (Hebrews 11:6).

"Those that seek me early will find me."
– (Proverbs 8:17).

"Let all those who seek thee rejoice."
– (Psalms 40:16).

These verses are simple and clear. God rewards those who seek him. For our prayers to be answered then, we must be born again. Additionally, believers must develop a hunger or passion for God. Song of Solomon 3:2 and 4 says:

"I must arise now and go to the city;

In the streets and in the squares

I must seek him whom my soul loves

I sought him but did not find him.

When I found him whom my soul loves,

I held onto him and would not let him go."

What will be the end of a careful and diligent search for God? *The true seeker will find him.* There are answers that need to be secured, petitions that need filling, truth to uncover, intimacies to engage, and an on-going relationship to build in seeking prayer. So, *seek him!*

Knocking prayer

The knocking prayer is prayer that seeks to open that which is closed. It refuses to take "no" for an answer. It discerns resistance and stands against it determinedly. Acts 12 records Herod's treatment of the disciples. He killed James, saw that it pleased the Jews, and decided to further appease them by having Peter arrested and imprisoned under a death sentence. Since Passover was nigh, Peter was imprisoned temporarily until that feast was finished (Acts 12:6).

One factor Herod and his cronies had not considered, however, was the power of Peter's praying friends. They did not sink into depression, quit, or lose faith in God. Just the contrary! They passionately responded to Peter's imprisonment by making, "prayer for him fervently"(Acts 12:6).

Peter's imprisonment was not symbolic, fictional, or a fantasy. His physical bondage was real, although not particularly unique. There are many examples of bondages in the Bible, especially among leaders. Hezekiah had failing health and worry; Ezra and Nehemiah had potent enemies; and Daniel was imprisoned. The man of Gadara was possessed by demons, the sinful woman (who washed

Jesus' feet with her hair) by lust, and Judas by greed. All prisons—whether actual, circumstantial, emotional, or physical, financial—mean bondage and some restraint on beneficial activity.

In Peter's case, knocking prayer was a request for a literal opening of the door of a real prison. Persistent, passionate praying catches the interest of God. Answering believing prayer is his delight. God sent his answer into Peter's prison in the form of an angel (Acts 12:7). This angelic being was more powerful than stone casements, heavy chains, and iron gates.

The angel gave Peter a three-part command: "get," "wrap," and "follow me." A light shone and Peter's circumstances changed in an instant. His gates were opened, the outer doors swung wide, and the angel led him freely to the street. God had responded to the prayer of knocking.

What about the people who were still praying and believing for an answer and for Peter's release? How would they respond? First, came unbelief, then wonderment, acceptance, and finally, joy. Rhoda, the housekeeper, was so thrilled to see Peter that she forgot to unlock the gate and let him in. She ran to the inner part of the house where the prayer meeting was in progress and announced to the group that Peter was at the door (Acts 12:13).

The Bible says they were amazed. I wonder why, since they were asking for precisely what was in progress before their eyes. In fairness to those folks, our contemporary response would likely be no different. Maybe they were amazed because they had little experience in answered prayer. Or perhaps, intellectually, it was just hard to receive such a quick and supernatural response from God.

Let us return to Rhoda at the unopened gate. When God answers, action is needed. When Peter knocked and Rhoda answered, the appropriate response would have been to let him in. Instead, in abandoned wonder or joy, or both, she went to report to her friends. Poor Peter! For him, answered prayer was one lock away. It is one concern when sinners or the world system restrains a person. It is quite another when you are locked out of your destiny by well meaning, God loving folks.

The response of Peter's prayer group is also noteworthy. The people did not believe Rhoda's report and kept praying, even though they had already received that for which they had been praying. They just did not believe God had answered.

Prayer for prayer's sake may have some intrinsic value, but I am not sure what that might be. Those who practice piano do not have as a final goal to be a good practicer. They practice to become a proficient performer. Those who pray do so to become a partner with God in releasing his Kingdom power on earth.

Prayer is always partnership with God. It goes far beyond telling God things he already knows. The prayer of knocking is one that continues in passion and persistence until there is a response from God. Peter's friends prayed until Peter was released back into their company. They won and so will you if you are persistent in prayer!

Resistance

What do you do when you "hit the wall" of resistance in prayer? Quit? Doubt? Pray once more and abandon the cause? Capitulate and let Satan triumph?

Check your heart motives. Why are you praying what you are praying? Is there potential for God to receive glory from your prayer? Is your heart clean before him? Answers can be blocked by unconfessed sin. Second, are you praying according to the will of God? Are you asking him rightly or amiss? Third, have you discerned what kind of resistance you are encountering? Is it a demon, the flesh, or people? Are you in spiritual warfare?

Timing and Circumstances

After one has determined the will of God in a prayer petition, the final matter in getting an answer relates to timing and circumstances. For example, many had prayed for centuries for Messiah to come. And yet, until the Greeks provided a common language for the Middle East and the Romans provided roads, postal and legal systems creating a culturally appropriate environment for the birth of Jesus, the Messiah could not come. Subsequent to the earthly ministry of Jesus, the apostles were able to send written epistles and to travel widely because of the Roman domination of the area. Timing! It is a matter of high priority in ministry and even more in prayer. Where do your prayers fit in as far as timing is concerned?

When an intercessor encounters resistance in

prayer, it is vital that he/she stay the course. Intercession is not the business of neophytes. The idea mentioned earlier of "praying through" is applicable here. The perceived need for an answer can, at times, override the need for continued knocking until an answer arrives. Don't let false perceptions interfere with your petitions. Keep knocking; pray on. In due season, that which has been blocked and closed to you will be fully opened.

Chapter Five
Prayer in God's Will

"For we don't know what we should pray for,
Nor how to pray as we should;
but the Holy Spirit prays for us with such feeling
that it cannot be expressed in words."
– Romans 8:26 (LB)

Romans 8:28 is among the most visited passages at prayer time. Strangely, this verse is also among the most misinterpreted in the New Testament. Misapplying Scripture from anywhere in the Bible takes away the power and effectiveness of the verses when misused and can lead to an unlimited number of erroneous conclusions.

The discussion of prayer and intercession from Romans 8 is widely read and the potential triumphs and victories therein are needed in our prayer pursuits and practice. However, the grossest misapplication of Romans 8 is centered in the usage and application of verse 28 which says, "We know God causes all things to work together for good to those who love God, to those who are called according to his purpose."

An often played game at children's birthday parties is "Pin the Tail on the Donkey." A child is blindfolded and led to a wall on which a poster of a donkey has been attached. The challenge is to pin the tail in the right location on the donkey. Most participants miss the spot and pin the tail on all locations on the donkey or on the wall, resulting in much laughter.

The Bible is used unwittingly in the same way. Christians have a game called "Pin The Verse On The Disaster" and Romans 8:28 is the verse most often used. From the well-intentioned hearts of sympathetic believers who want to comfort the hurting comes the "all things work together for good" phrase. The Bible has many verses that speak about comfort, but verse 28 is not one of them. The consequences of this misapplication can cause a person to think wrongly about God as well as their situation. Comfort is not found in the context of Romans 8:22-28. Prayer and intercession are!

Let us review the verses preceding verse 28 to determine what Paul was teaching the Roman believers. You will notice in verse 22 that the "whole creation groans," then in verse 23, "we ourselves groan." Paul personally identifies with the Roman believers in their "groaning". That term emanates from childbirth.

Paul continued to teach and explain to the Romans why their praying was so weak. They did not know how to pray "as is necessary." We will find out what that means later, but what is important to know now is that the consequence of not praying as is necessary resulted in fruitless lives and a powerless church. Amazingly, the Holy Spirit came into their weak praying to define and qualify their request and empower them.

There is zero prayer power apart from the assistance of the Holy Spirit because, first and foremost, the Holy Spirit is God. He will, therefore, always be concerned with fulfilling the Father's purposes. Second, and critical to all who pray, God knows the mind of the Spirit. Thus he prays according to knowledge. That is why Holy Spirit led and empowered prayer is absolutely essential and so powerful.

Asking Correctly

Why do we not "pray as is necessary"? There are at least two reasons. First, there is the matter of our humanness. When someone is suffering and asks for our prayers, our emotions sympathetically jump to the need before we give our spirit an opportunity to make an inquiry of the Lord.

Second, we often pray with partial or inadequate knowledge because we have only a human appraisal of a situation. *Therefore, we do not know how to pray because we have not discerned how or what to pray!* In the absence of understanding God's intentions, we pray out of our human understanding. Prayer in this instance becomes little more than an exercise of the flesh propelled by passionate sympathies. However, praying in God's will is different. He is not bound to respond to flesh-generated prayers, no matter how well-intentioned they are or how much they are needed.

Some years ago I met with a group of ladies in my church, at their request, for a mid-day prayer meeting and to give some instruction on prayer and intercession. I read the core text from Romans 8 that we are studying in this chapter. Afterwards, I had a sense that God was going to do something special – and he did! That prayer meeting became a laboratory for the Holy Spirit to teach us about God-illuminated intercession. All who attended had their prayer lives changed profoundly.

In the midst of a general discussion about the verses we had read, an associate pastor placed a written prayer request in my lap and walked away without comment. It was a request to pray for a lady well known in our church who had just received a medical report saying she had a life-threatening illness. The ladies wanted to immediately plunge into death-rebuking and demon-chasing prayer. I felt a hesitation and asked that they not do that. "How do we know," I asked, "that the diagnosis she received is correct or that the lady even has that disease at all?"

One lady heatedly protested my advice, insisting that since one of our leaders had a terminal disease the situation demanded immediate and forceful prayer. I did not say that we shouldn't pray or wouldn't pray. I only said I did not feel at liberty to pray for the condition announced to us until I had an answer to a nagging question, "How, Lord, should we pray about this need?"

After the lady calmed down, she admitted that my words made sense and everyone present agreed that they were willing to try asking God for wisdom before we did anything else. We knelt by our chairs and almost immediately the Holy Spirit whispered something in my ear about the ill woman. I wrote it down on the prayer request slip that had been handed to me.

None of us were prepared for what happened next. The lady who was so fervent about praying began to weep uncontrollably and pray from deep within with groans and sounds no language can define and only God fully understands. After a few moments, with eyes closed, and emotionally, she began to speak of an episode from the life of the person who was ill. Speaking as though this lady was present, the intercessor spoke of seeing a man trying to accost and kidnap the woman when she was a young girl. She saw the girl screaming and kicking and the man running away. She then saw something like a fishnet woven with large cords coming down and covering the body of the girl. On every cord was written the words "the spirit of fear."

As we continued in prayer, each lady present had a visual insight into some segment of the ill lady's life, and in every segment the words, "the spirit of fear" appeared. On the paper handed to me, I had also written "the spirit of fear." We had a sevenfold witness.

All this happened during a Wednesday lunch hour and it was also the day on which our midweek service was held. That evening, after a short time of worship, I called the lady and her husband to the front and explained to them the events of the lunch hour prayer time. As a congregation we prayed over them without mentioning the disease the doctors had diagnosed. Why did we not mention what the doctors had said? Because the only information we had from the Holy Spirit spoke of the spirit of fear and it was against that spirit we prayed.

The next day the lady went to the hospital for three days of testing. No trace of her life-threatening disease was found. The reason why? It was not there to begin with! She did not have the disease diagnosed by the doctor. Even the symptoms of the disease had gone.

Since she did not have the disease diagnosed by her doctor, even if our prayer group had prayed all day long, she still would be having her symptoms. She would not have been helped. As a prayer group, we would have asked amiss. We would have been asking God to do something where no action was required.

Even more important, the real condition–the spirit of fear–would have gone undetected and would not have received prayer at all. There would have been failure on every front. The intercessors, the ill lady, and our human centered prayers would not have worked. The Holy Spirit could not have done his work in this instance because no one had asked for specific information from him. As a point of interest, my wife and I recently saw the lady mentioned in this story. She is in perfect health and has been for a number of years.

May I confess something? Until the time of this incident, I believe most of my prayers were prayers "amiss." Here's why I believe that. For the most part, they were generated from the soul and by-passed the leadership of the Holy Spirit. Little wonder, then, that so few of my prayers were being answered.

Few of our prayers are prayed in emergency situations, very few! As a rule, we have time to be thoughtful and reflective in prayer. It would be an overstatement to say there is a second agenda to every prayer need. However, even if we know from the Holy Spirit *how* to pray, we still need the assistance to know *what* to pray.

Write these questions at the top of your prayer list and put them before your prayer groups. When requests are received, say to the Lord at the beginning of your prayers, 'How do you want me to pray about this? What do I need to know to pray effectively for this request?" Stay with your inquiry until you have an answer. Only when you have knowledge from God can an effective, direct prayer be made because then you have the mind of Christ. You are praying God's will and his purposes. We cannot pray effectively with anticipation of an answer without an impartation of God's wisdom. We should be grateful that this kind of information is available and we should access it at every opportunity.

Take a moment to re-read Romans 8:22-28. Notice in verse 22 the phrase "the whole creation groans and suffers the pains of childbirth." In the following verses the word groan is used twice–in verse 23 speaking of Paul joining the Roman Christians and groaning within, and verse 26 of the Holy Spirit who "intercedes for us with groanings too deep for words."

Several things in these verses are mentioned as suffering and in need of relief. The first is the created world. What started in perfection as a garden called Eden was blighted by the introduction of sin through Adam and Eve. The second are the saints at Rome who yearn for political relief as well as the coming of the Lord. The third call for help is from those who pray. It is astonishing and encouraging that the Holy Spirit has become a co-sufferer in intercession. The first and second set of "groaners" has a there-and-then sense about them. The intercessors have a here-and-now sense!

Taken in its entirety, Romans 8:22-28 is a passage depicting the possibilities and benefits of things released by intercession. The idea of all things working together for good makes sense only when the "all things" are the result of penetrating intercession. Everything God sends in answer to intercession does work for the benefit of his people. Certainly there are other things that come into our lives as intruders but not those things that come from him. He is a Father and his intent is to benefit his children.

The altar of intercession is the place of conception in the love of God. It is the place where God plants his desires in our hearts and spirits. It is a private place of nurturing righteous desires with tears, time, and attention, without public promotion or view. Likewise, answers to prayer are often unseen, sometimes for years. We know something good is happening, even though we do not know exactly what. Then, suddenly, God shows what he had planned all along.

As a child is conceived, so are the ways of God in intercession. Children are normally the consequence of an act between a man and his wife. The fetus in the womb continues unseen by the world for nine months. The changes in the body of the mother are the only visible sign that something is happening inwardly. Everyone knows something is alive and growing. That is no secret. But *what that is remains to be seen.*

In a normal pregnancy, the nine-month timeline brings with it the reality of the birth moment. In that birth moment, powerful contractions and pain grip the mother and, after a period of time, a child is birthed for everyone to see and enjoy. After the arrival of the child, few people, including the mother, pay any attention to the stress and pressure required to produce the child.

Gloria and I are the parents of four children, three sons and a daughter. I was able to be present when three of the four were born. The delivery room was hectic, scary, painful for my wife, and absolutely spectacular–all at the same time! No amount of instruction or preparation can thoroughly prepare a person for the emotional stretch that is demanded by the entrance of a new child. Then, into the midst of the delivery room frenzy, a new life appears and with it comes joy.

Intercession is labor intensive, love filled, and motivated (see James 5). The ground of intercession is often moistened with tears as God's purposes, his will, and his plans are being nurtured both in the heavenly realms and in the human heart. At the appropriate time, those plans burst forth like a sudden surprise.

Our praying needs help! We need to become focused in "Thy kingdom come [and] thy will be done" (Matthew 6:10 KJV). Our prayers need the aid and assistance of the Holy Spirit to sort out our true heart motives, to discern self serving desires, to comprehend the purposes of God. Romans 8:23 is the key to understanding the help the Holy Spirit provides. *Most importantly, he intercedes for us according to the will of God*

Look again at Romans 8:28. "And we know God causes all things [that are conceived in intercessory prayer assisted and prompted by the Holy Spirit] to work together for good" (my paraphrase). As a corollary, let's add in what Jesus said in John 16:24. "Until now you have asked for nothing in my name; ask, and you will receive, that your joy may be full."

Chapter Six
Fasting

"Prayer is, above all, a means of forming character.
It combines freedom and power with service and love."

– Dallas Willard

"The humble shall see their God at work for them."

– Psalm 69:32 LB

His dream had come true. A local church youth minister and his largely unmotivated youth group had prayed and God answered in a special way. Hundreds of young people began to stream to the weekly youth services. Hundreds were converted, delivered from drugs and sex addictions; others were reconciled with parents and began to live radical Christian lives. It was a very special time in the life of that church.

After enduring large crowds and packed facilities for almost three years, the youth pastor decided to start a parachurch youth ministry with an outreach focus. He interviewed the very best actors, dramatists, singers, dancers, and instrumentalists. Naturally, he wanted top talent on his team. But the real beginning did not come from the acceptance of his call by the dancers and singers. It came through the life of a single young lady who had only one talent. *She knew how to pray!*

One day, this young lady came to interview for a ministry position. She was not gifted in speaking, singing, or playing music. In fact, she did not like being in front of crowds. She was a bit overweight and had a skin condition on her face. When she asked about a staff position in the new ministry the leader responded by asking, "What can you do?" After a short interview she was turned away with little hope. A few days later she returned and the results were the same. There were no openings for her. She made several more attempts the leader finally asked out of his desperation, "Isn't there anything you can do?" "Yes, I can pray," she quietly replied. The leader instructed her to go pray thinking that would end her desire to serve. It didn't. She began to pray in earnest about this proposed new ministry, and she began to fast. Her fasting went on for a week, and then another. Finally, forty-two days passed while she fasted and prayed. At the end of that time, there was a spiritual explosion so great it launched a ministry that became national in scope. It proved the fact that fasting does accomplish some very important things.

In a country like America where a large percentage of the population is overweight, where eating is part of the national pastime, where the diet industry does billions in business annually, the idea of denying food intake for spiritual purposes is not popular. While I am grateful for my upbringing and rich spiritual heritage, I do feel I lack in training in some areas of the Christian disciplines and fasting is one of them. Jesus often fasted, one time for forty days. Fasting was a regular part of the Jewish belief system.

On one occasion, Jesus corrected some Jews on the practice, but not for the fasting; he chastised them for their prideful exhibitions over it:

> *"And whenever you fast, do not put on a gloomy face as the hypocrites do, for they neglect their appearance in order to be seen fasting by men. Truly I say to you, they have their reward in full! But you, when you fast, anoint your head, and wash your face so that you may not be seen fasting by men, but your Father who is in secret; and your Father who sees in secret will repay you."* – (Matthew 6:16-18)

Through the entire Bible, fasting is linked to prayer. Jesus did not terminate or limit fasting, but he did call for humility of heart as the proper condition for it. To be beneficial, fasting must be birthed from a heart that is in right relationship to God and clothed in humility.

Twice in my life I have been led to lengthy fasts. Both were seasons of profound and significant dealing in my life. Normally, in January of each year I spend a few days in special prayer and fasting. The focus of that time is to refresh my heart and spirit, to become more sensitive to God, and to find a sense of what God may be emphasizing or saying specifically in the coming months. Those times have, without exception, been productive.

Fasting is a spiritual discipline that the Christian world needs to rediscover. Donald Whitney defines fasting as a "Christian's voluntary absence from food for spiritual purpose."[1] Abstaining from such a fashionable and pleasurable matter as food has a hard sound to it. Yet it is an integral part of the call to discipleship, which is first and foremost a call to deny oneself. Whitney says, "Christians in a gluttonous, denial-less, self indulgent society may struggle to accept and begin the practice of fasting."[2] Yet, apart from deliberate self denial emanating from a heart of love, we cannot be called disciples of Jesus.

The root of the word translated "to fast" means "to afflict the soul" or "to deny oneself." Denial of any kind is nearly unknown in Western churches today. The opposite should be true. Awards go to the blessing seekers. Dallas Willard says, "Fasting is one of the more important ways of practicing self denial required of anyone who would follow Jesus."[3]

In Western culture, food is idolized. Likewise, in most churches the term "fellowship" does not equate with Bible study or prayer or meaningful discussions about God. It almost *always* involves food consumption. Willard says, "Since food has the pervasive place it does in our lives, the effects of fasting will be diffused through our personalities."

Encouragements to eat and overindulge are many. To promote fasting as a spiritual discipline is to stand against the culture itself. Because food is needed for basic survival, its abuse is usually hidden. The restaurants that survive are those that serve the largest portions. Every form of cultural event involves food. Could it be that the "belly" has become the god of our culture? Self denial and self control in the area of eating must become part of the discipleship cost of following Jesus.

Fasting is voluntary. It is obedience to God's pattern for the Christian life. Fasting is normative. For those physically able, both the Old and New Testament present fasting as an expected behavior. It is part of learning and practicing self denial. The increased spiritual capacities that result from fasting are required for ministry now and will be even more so in the future. Fasting is required in emergency situations. Remember the incident with the sons of Sceva in the New Testament? (See Acts 19:14-ff) The demons would not depart except through fasting and prayer.

In the ancient world, locating food and preparing it occupied a major portion of the day. In our contemporary world, busyness steals just as much time. One key ingredient in fasting is that the time normally used for food preparation and consumption gets redirected to intercession. In today's world, time has a higher value than money. We cannot find more time; we can only make better use of the time we have. Among the strongest and first challenges to developing a successful prayer life will be the allocation of time for prayer and reflection. There are many time robbers and hour thieves and you will get well acquainted with them when you determine to have a disciplined, regular prayer time.

Time usually taken up in food preparation, consumption, and clean up can be reallocated to prayer and intercession–the kind of prayer that seeks intimacy with God. This must be the first motive for all fasting. Fasting does not coerce God into doing things or speed up his response time. No! But fasting does draw us closer to his heart. Fasting will vacate time blocs for prayer.

Preparing for a Fast

Persons entering a time of fasting must give due diligence to their bodies. Soda, coffee, and tea drinkers usually develop headaches because of caffeine withdrawal. If you have health problems, or if you are a senior saint, your doctor should be consulted before you begin any fast longer than one or two meals.

Food consumption should be restricted for a few days prior to a lengthy fast, with meat products stopped altogether. Stick to fruit and vegetables and lots of water. The day before you begin a fast, you may want to drink only water and bouillon or broth. Many long-term fasters drink only water and juices. Many commercially produced and widely available juices are full of refined sugars, so read the labels beforehand. Water is better than any other liquid.

The body requires a few days to purify, cleanse, and expel the toxins we've fed into it. While every person's body is slightly different, somewhere between the sixth and tenth day the desire for food will subside and will remain quiet for many days. The days after the appetite has been suppressed are the best days of a fast. One characteristic of such a lengthy fast is increased sensitivity to the Holy Spirit. Fresh empowerment is another. Fasting also assists the prayer life and opens the heart and mind to probes of God. Observe the authority operating in Jesus' life during his forty day fast (Matthew 4:1-11).

Summary

All the matters above, by themselves, are worthy

reasons to fast, but they are not singularly or collectively the prime reason. The prime reason is best stated in the words of Lou Engle: "In fasting we are not trying to get something from God, but are seeking to align our hearts with his." [4]

The insatiable, constant, running-after-strange-gods heart of man has trouble coming under the rule of God because it is capable of a simultaneous multitude of competing loves and affections. How can all these emotions be brought under control? Fasting is one of the primary ways to deal with man's deepest drive–survival–and food is related to that. Fasting as a practice over a few days will yield great benefits, and is one of the key means of receiving from God.

The soul, made up of the mind, emotions, and will is the most trouble prone and resistant to change. It is also the most misunderstood, the most capable of being bruised by life's activities, and the most able to remember and sustain pain from hurts. In sum, the soul is powerful. Fasting, accompanied by commiserate praying, quiets bodily appetites, enhances sensitivity of our spirit, and opens the soul to God.

A Call To Fast

May I encourage you to fast? Start by abstaining from food for one meal once a week. Use your meal time for a short Bible study and some specific praying. Then listen to what he may say. If we draw near to him, he has promised to draw near in return.

Chapter Seven
About Intercessors

*"The prayers of the saints are the capital stock of heaven
by which God carries on His great work upon the earth."*
—E. M. Bounds

Intercessors are among the least noticed but most
valued persons in God's work. They are hard to find,
challenging to train, and demanding to look after. They
are marked by God and have special grace to remain
prayerful for years over important matters should that
need be required. Because they feel just a bit of what God
feels, they care very much—perhaps at times even in a
protective way—about the interests of God. Intercessors
are identified by the following characteristics:

Intercessors pray on behalf of others. The "others"
may be God or people because both have needs to fulfill.
God has needs? Yes! He needs people to partner with him
in the release of Kingdom power and purposes on the
earth. And, of course, the needs of humans are immense
since we live in a cursed world and declining universe.

Intercessors are intense and passionate. Tears and
passion are marks that distinguish intercessors. They live

to see the plans and purposes of God released in the earth and deal with the gap between heaven and earth on a regular basis. They care so much about God's concerns that they occasionally may seem a bit too heavenly minded. True intercessors are intense because God's concerns in heaven and earth depend upon their prayers. A deep passion for God and righteousness motivates them. Intercessors live before the face of God.

Intercessors are sensitive. It is the business of intercessors to hear God's voice and, from that hearing, to pray for his purposes to be accomplished. The Bible says, "He who has an ear, let him hear" (Revelation 2:7 NIV). The clear inference is that some people hear better in prayer than others. Those with this capability are commanded to listen to what he is saying through his Spirit, and to allow what they hear to settle into their spirits. Intercession is a response to listening. This is a characteristic that needs to be much encouraged and developed. There is great value in having people in prayer ministries who are sensitive to God's voice and who know how to discern God's voice from the many that clamor for attention.

Intercessors are forceful and persuasive. Warfare with demonic spirits is a part of intercession, and intercessors are not ones to shy away from a battle. They are known for their determination and doggedness. Pastors do well to remember that intercessors do not cease being forceful and persuasive when they finish praying. They have become who and what they are in part because of time spent in God's presence and because of the intercession anointing that rests on them. Intercessors are called and willing to deal with the spirit realm; however, leaders will be called upon to deal with them on the human plain.

Intercessors are usually under attack. There are two activities that invite attacks from hell more than any others. The first is evangelism. Soul winners are depopulating hell and populating heaven and the devil doesn't like it. The second activity that invites attack is intercession. Why? Because, by its nature, intercession confronts evil in the spirit realm. Leaders over intercessors should be advised they will be dealing with people under perpetual attack.

The Bible tells us that Satan is the "prince and power of the air." Intercessors, by their praying, cut through the air space inhabited by demons and evil spirits–usurpers who are not quick to yield turf or territory. Intercession shakes them, attacks them head on, disturbs and jars their work, and seeks their immediate return to hell from whence they came. Occupying a place, person, or space on earth is vastly more enjoyable to them than being locked in hell. Their general assignment, like Satan's himself, is to "steal, rob and destroy" (see John 10:10). The intent of Jesus is just the opposite. He provides "life and life more abundantly." Thus, we see the reason for conflict.

Intercessors and Congregational Life

Intercessors need time and a place to pray beyond the normal flow of church services. Small groups meeting in prayer chapels and homes provide a good environment. Separation from the main congregation is needed but, at the same time, pastors must ensure that elitism is resisted. Hard work is required to maintain the balance.

Intercessors should not, and cannot, control a Sunday service for prayer purposes as these are typically for worship, teaching, and fellowship. However, intercessors play an important role in setting the stage for everything that happens in those public services. First, they pray for the meetings *before* they happen. Some churches have rotating teams that pray *while* the preaching is going on. During prayer times or at the end of a service, these persons are available for prayer, although that is a different level than deep intercession.

Prophetic Intercessors

Because intercessors are diligent about seeking God's face, they can–better than others–discern the true nature of a thing being prayed for, as well as the potential solution. Many intercessors have a secondary gifting in the prophetic realm.

Prophetic intercessors are a challenge to work with because they tend to see things in black and white; there is no gray, no in-between. Furthermore, when they "see" they expect those in leadership to take immediate action– if nothing else, to at least make a declaration of what God said. Thus, it is of highest importance that those who intercede with prophetic anointings and those who lead them develop a grid of understanding. They need a framework that allows information to come to the leadership to be processed as to timing, content, and interpretation. The leadership needs to consider how and when to respond, and whether it is appropriate to be shared with the congregation.

Intercessors must also understand that the majority

of things revealed to them are for the purpose of further prayer and not for public discourse or congregational distribution. They must also understand confidentiality. They must understand how to practice listening to "all things and holding fast to that which is good." Leaders who develop a cadre of prophetic intercessors will be on their way to a healthier church and more influential ministry in their communities.

Intercessors need refreshing and special attention

Because of frequent attacks, intercessors need times of refreshing and encouragement. A veteran minister friend of mine planned a retreat twice a year just for the intercessors of his church. During those times they were instructed not to pray for anyone or anything except in their personal devotions. The weekends were designed for rest and refreshing. As a result of this action, the pastor had more than three hundred intercessors in his church who continued strong and resilient year after year.

Military leaders know well the value of rest and refreshing. During the Vietnam conflict, leaders of the American forces sent troops out of the war zone for a few days of what was called R and R, or rest and recuperation. War is intense, dangerous, and exhausting. Without proper rest, the soldiers lose their edge. It is the same for intercessors who are waging a spiritual war. Pastors need to be careful as to how they treat them and must develop a plan to nurture them.

What do intercessors need? Care. Attention. Training. Leading. Development. A special place to pray.

The best intercession is done away from crowds, even church crowds. Intercessors also need trust and confidence in their ability to hear and keep sacred information that is just that–sacred. Also, intercessors themselves need prayer. Church leaders need to keep the needs of the intercessors before the congregation. If intercessors receive appropriate instruction, a private place for ministry, and trust from their leaders, great gain can be garnered from their ministry.

Intercessors! Respect them and lift them to God often. They hold the world together with their prayers.

Chapter Eight
The Prayer Gathering

"Seek first his kingdom and his righteousness."
– Matthew 6:33

The largest prayer mobilization in church history is now in progress. If the actual number of people praying were counted, that number would be the highest in history. Inestimable good is being done through multiple prayer efforts and much more will follow because God loves prayer and praying brings divine rewards.

Why the high profile prayer emphasis? Is it a fad? A *cause celebre?* No! *The worldwide prayer emphasis comes from God.* He is calling his people to a cooperative partnership with him. The call has several parts: heart purification, Spirit filling, and then partnership in prayer.

It is through prayer that Kingdom power and purpose are released on earth. Remember the model prayer Jesus gave his disciples? Part of that prayer says, "Thy kingdom come. Thy will be done on earth as it is in heaven" (Matthew 6:10).

Prayer is not a blue sky, fantasy-seeking enterprise. There is a very real and tangible here-and-now sense and on-the-earth effect to prayer. The full dimensions of such prayer have not yet been fully seen. They are far more numerous than we know, more expansive than we have imagined.

Personal Prayer

Discipline as well as a time and place are required to grow a successful prayer life. If we do not have a specific time and place, we probably will not pray regularly or effectively. Everything in life we deem important has a time demand in relationship to its importance. What about prayer? What about God's needs? What about the needs of the world? What about power for evangelizing? What about our families? Do these matters require time and attention from us? Are they worthy of the investment? Of course they are!

Where can we get help? There is a plethora of daily devotional guides in any Christian bookstore and in many secular ones as well. Find one that works with you and for you. Use anything that will discipline, systematize, shape and enliven your prayer time. The following is a simple guide you can use every day and almost anywhere to develop structure in your personal prayer time.

- Open with worship.

- Read scriptures slowly and carefully (more for meaning than quantity).

- Ask for cleansing.

- Ask how he wants you to pray.

- Make petitions and requests.

- Listen for God's voice (usually a quiet inward prompting).
- Write down what you hear (obey quickly if God sends an order).
- Worship and give thanks.
- Develop your prayer time until it becomes a life giving habit!

Corporate Prayer Gatherings

There are many types of corporate prayer gatherings, including prayer concerts, assemblies, days of repentance and humiliation, and national and local days of prayer. It is my heartfelt belief that personal prayer times need to be coupled with corporate (group) praying in any context.

Strength comes in numbers. Much good is being done across the world through specific prayer targeted towards the lost. Peter Wagner's *Prayer Mobilization for the Nations*, Cindy Jacob's *Intercessors for America*, and Ed Silvosa's *Lighthouses of Prayer* are a few of the larger and more visible prayer ministries. These, and others like them, are having an impact on the world.

Lively, well-led, prayer specific, corporate intercessory gatherings are much needed. Prayer gatherings express dependence upon God. It is a time when we pray together about mutual concerns. Unfortunately, there are genuine enemies of corporate prayer gatherings. The big three are mental distractions, talking, and excessive need sharing. These challenges also affect one's personal prayer life along with one giant enemy–sleep!

Sleep and Its Antidote

A new attendee came to a church I once pastored. Full of excitement and enthusiasm, he expressed his interest in prayer and thought we should have a church-wide, all-night prayer meeting. Knowing what a challenge it is for me to pray well for an hour, to stay focused for an entire night seemed Herculean. Seven or eight hours of straight prayer? Whew! Would we be called "prayer warriors" if we lived through this? Would the warfare be against Satan or our flesh?

A few weeks later I reluctantly agreed to the request and an extended prayer meeting was scheduled from 9 P.M. until 5 A.M. A break was scheduled at 1 A.M. for a check up and a time of refreshing. From my perspective, the break was planned to see how people looked after trying to pray for four and half hours, and with almost that much time remaining.

The prayer group gathered in our church prayer room. Our young newcomer started to pray and pray loud. Very loud indeed! He was so loud he was soon the sole occupant of our prayer room as the rest of us scattered about the church to find a place of quiet so we could focus our prayers. From time to time I walked around the church campus to be sure everyone was comfortable, to answer any questions or to agree with someone in need.

By 10:30 P.M. the prayer room was quiet. Through an open door, I saw our young man on a couch fast asleep and snoring loud enough to keep demons at bay. He slept the rest of the night. *His mistake was getting too comfortable in his prayer posture.* The rest of us paced up and down, sat upright and erect or just leaned against the church walls. We stayed awake because of our posture.

If you get too comfortable during prayer, you may find yourself in the same condition. You will not pray for long if you are lying flat on your back or in your favorite easy chair. I have seen people sleeping while leaning over the altar rail at the front of a church.

How can you conquer the sleep problem? Stand up to pray. Pray while pacing back and forth. If you fall asleep from these positions, it will become for you a memorial in your prayer life. By standing and pacing, your body requires more oxygen. Walking deepens breathing and circulation and this stimulates alertness.

Talking and Protracted Need Sharing

Talking and extensive need sharing are negatives that seriously dilute the power and effectiveness of a prayer gathering. The verbalization of prayer needs at the beginning of a meeting devastates faith. In dozens of prayer services I have attended, the need sharing starts, then is embellished, then someone forgot a detail (always important stuff, of course), then others release more details until the weight of human need and distress is so overwhelming, that faith withers. If you are not careful, a simple request to pray for an ill person can easily become a verbal vehicle for their life-long medical history, generational sins, a list of their medical advisors, reports of the family black sheep, their last vacation destination, and the winner of last year's Little League baseball competition.

If you are in a prayer meeting and listen to thirty or forty minutes of needs, and I admit that many of them will be important, your faith and ability to pray can be negatively impacted. When your mind is loaded with needs before it is centered on Jesus, it will be hard to pray in a faith-filled, effective way. Remember this chorus?

Turn your eyes upon Jesus
Look full in His wonderful face
And the things of earth will grow strangely dim
In the light of your glory and grace.
– Helen Howarth Lemmel

It is appropriate and needful to make our requests known to God. However, these needs should not become the center of a prayer time. Jesus must always be the center.

How can we have better prayer services? Start with a chorus or two and then have a time of hearty praise. You could add a testimony of recently answered prayer. Then, when there is a conscious sense of God being present, that is the time to lift requests to God. After a lengthy season in God's presence, making petitions is an easy matter.

Selfish Praying

Furthermore, our prayers need to be centered in "Thy kingdom come [and] thy will be done." As mentioned in Chapter 4, start by asking God how to pray about a matter. Praying God's will and praying with wisdom is the starting point of effective praying. It will lift us from the zone of self-centered, personal pursuits to engage the things important to God.

Wandering thoughts

Yet another enemy of effective praying is wandering thoughts. There are few points at which the thoughts tend to be more non-focused and wander further into a mental no-man's-land than at the point of prayer. The "soulical" part of man (mind, emotions, will) has the capacity to engage in innumerable thought streams simultaneously. Anyone who has prayed has had the personal challenge to bring "every thought captive to the obedience of Christ" (2 Corinthians 10:5).

I am not exempt from this challenge and the frustration it brings in trying to pray effectively. Often at the start of prayer, such things as accumulated thoughts, people who need attention, our overseas work, family concerns, and many other matters fill my mind. It is natural, but it is still one of the major challenges to prayer. A mind is not a mind unless thoughts run through it, so how can we get it under control? Disciplining the thought life is a victory yet to be won in many lives. Can a normally functioning mind with its torrents of thoughts be converted, disciplined, and controlled to focus on God and his interests? Yes, but it takes work and hard work at that.

Several things can be done to help concentration. First, pray aloud. Let your ears hear what your heart is saying. Second, pray the word of God. God's word is the mind of Christ and the expressed will of God. Third, stay with steps one and two until you have a keen and clear conscious sense of God's presence. Then you can verbalize requests easily.

Leadership

Local prayer gatherings need leaders with sensitive spirits to guide prayer meetings. These services should never be dominated by one or two people or by the volume of one or two. They must be conducted by a person led by the Holy Spirit and must not be driven or dominated.

In the church of my childhood, there was an elder who often looked after the prayer services. He was mightily used of God to keep a flow, and he was able to lovingly but firmly keep potential dominators in check. The leader must be able to discern "where" a meeting is and "where" it should be going.

Prayer leaders must be trained and anointed. They must keep focused on everything said and done. Prayer leaders must be discipled and periodically monitored for effectiveness.

Spiritually mature Christians are needed in this position since prayer and intercession are the jugular of the church.

Making it All Come Together

What is the best kind of prayer service? It is the one that works in your environment, the one in which the people are comfortable with the leadership, the one in which everyone can freely participate, and the one in which the people actually touch God. Nothing else is really important!

All the modes mentioned above and dozens more are needed at one time or another. General prayer concerns must, of necessity, be mingled with personal requests and needs into which the entire prayer group can partner in intercession.

A prayer group leader could facilitate thirty or forty minutes of corporate prayer followed by a few minutes of individual requests handled on a one-by-one basis. By these means, the entire group can participate and add strength by praying in agreement.

Reality Check

Every prayer event needs a periodic reality check. What happened as a result of our praying? It helps to keep a prayer log listing both requests and answers by date. Endless praying without confirmation of answers leads to frustration and bewilderment. Make answered prayer a public matter. Let everyone know what God has done, especially those who prayed.

Summary

Prayer meetings are back! They can be wonderful, alive, and effective if you, the leader, take time to train workers in the specifics of handling and creating good meetings. They can be positive and meaningful if there is a high level of participation in the meetings themselves. They can be attractive if you advertise what God has done as a result of intercession. And they can be faith building from on-going testimonials. Let's get praying!

Chapter Nine
Spiritual Warfare and Intercession

"The weapons of our warfare are not carnal."
−2 Corinthians 10:4

This chapter is short. The reasons? First, the Bible has little to show by example or say in principle about the subject of spiritual warfare. Secondly, I want to state in writing my willingness to be corrected on this subject and my need to know more about warfare as it relates to intercession. But from a point of logic, if God wanted us to be specialists in spiritual warfare, one could conclude that he would have made all that explicit in his Word. For instance, *there are four gospels*. The message of salvation cannot be missed. But the current spiritual warfare stuff could easily be. Apparently intercession has more to do with releasing Kingdom life than ridiculing demon spirits; more to do with creating life than chasing our spiritual nemesis; more to do with the superiority and centrality of Jesus than attacks on Jezebel's minions.

Let me be very clear. I do believe in a literal devil that has some permitted powers in the universe. What I struggle with is how much time and attention he deserves in the context of our prayer lives. As you know, spiritual warfare teaching and conferences are popular today. Huge conferences are held focusing on casting down strongholds over cities and regions. If there is measurable evidence that those strongholds and demons have been overthrown, I think it should be published for everyone's encouragement. To date, and hopefully I'll soon have to rewrite this section because of increased revelation or empirical proof, no nation or city has been converted en-masse.

When one views videos and hears reports of God's working in various places, it is easy to mentally extrapolate a bigger result than what actually occurred. Those conclusions are not necessarily the fault of the writers or producers. They are the consequences of religious hopes and imaginations not entirely based in reality.

One overly enthused American minister landed in Delhi, India. When he had descended the plane stairs onto the tarmac he knelt down, pope-like, and kissed the ground. Then he uttered this amazing statement: "I cast the spirit of Hinduism out of India." Did his words really get that deed done? The year was 1983. Has Hinduism diminished one bit since then?

Another well-regarded leader led thousands of worshippers at a prayer event in a Muslim nation. Near the end of that gathering he announced, "The evil forces over this region have been cast down." Really? In reality, there are more Muslims there now than before his highly applauded announcement, and the current Muslims seem to have a more militant attitude. His words did something, but that "something" had unexpected negative consequences. The public railing against Satan actually stirred him to bring increasing hostilities on God's people. The "inferred" consequence of the demonic confrontation, that is, casting Satan down and out of the country, simply did not happen.

In a meeting in which I was present along with seven thousand others, the leader said, "We have cast down the spirit of physical assaults and murder. They have been cast into hell." Would it not have been a great thing if what had been announced actually happened? Sadly it did not. My interest was piqued so I requested and kept crime statistics from the city where the meeting had been held. When I checked thirteen months after the devil rebuking, foot stomping (Satan is under our feet you know), and yelling into the air meeting, the crime statistics were appalling. Physical assaults were up thirty-five percent and murders were up twenty-two percent. What happened? We know for sure what did not happen. Murder and physical assaults are still on the loose or at the end of a very elastic tether.

In fairness, it should be noted that as far as can be known, all the persons referenced above are people of good intention and character. They seem to believe what they are doing is making a difference. But is it? And if it is, how do you know that? Is mapping the spirit world possible and can it be accurate? And after you have a "map" what then can be done with it? If one knows all the demons that occupy the earth, I can't see where that information has more potential than knowing the Father's heart.

Soul winning is the primary New Testament means

to defeat Satan's efforts on planet earth. In that process people are taken from the Kingdom of darkness to the Kingdom of light. Soul winning as a primary life focus seems scripturally sound, spiritually affirming, Jesus centered and transformational. You might be asking, "What about the powers of the devil?" And I say, "what about them?" Are we to be consumed with a Satan centered lifestyle? Again, it's a personal perception, but those who are consumed with demon powers and strategies do not seem to be active, engaging soul winners or intercessors. I wonder why?

I am still looking in the New Testament for a theological framework on which to hang the practices currently afloat in spiritual warfare circles. In the New Testament, there are only three places where warfare is mentioned.

There is mention of warfare in the following texts:

- 1 Corinthians 9:7: The context speaks of soldiers who fight deserving pay.

- 1 Timothy 1:18: Paul instructs Timothy towards faithfulness and to war or to contend for the faith since some have wandered away.

- 2 Corinthians 10:4: This verse speaks of weapons of war not being carnal. The object of the fight rests in the struggles in one's thought life.

Demons are not mentioned in any of the above verses directly or by inference.

Is Ephesians 6:11-20 about spiritual warfare as it is commonly imagined in contemporary Christian circles? These verses describe the protection that believers have against demonic principalities and powers which wage war in the heavenly realms. The context does not indicate in any way that believers should be on a verbal offensive against Satan. And yet the method of warfare so popular today seems to mainly consist of yelling commands and rebukes at Satan. The text clearly indicates that a Christian is protected from demonic power, that protection is applied by personal choices ("put on"), and draws its strength by actively engaging in intercession. Ephesians 6:18 instructively indicates all believers who want to be protected should, "pray at all times in the Spirit" and "with all perseverance and petition for all the saints." Clearly the direction of the activity is not spiritual warfare as practiced today in our country. Paul's instruction is to protect oneself from Satan. One major way to do that is to pray insistently in the power of the Holy Spirit.

2 Corinthians 10:4 is used as the primary scripture to defend the lambasting demons by any and all means. Jesus did say that he was in possession of "all power in heaven and earth" (Matthew 28:18). Because of what he possesses and makes available to believers, we who follow him already have authority to "cast out demons" (Mark 16:17). We can't hope for more and we don't need less.

What does bring a change in a home, community and church? Praying people do! When people pray consistently and insistently and then live out the life of God that flows from that in a Holy Spirit and scripturally defined way, changes occur at every level. Communities are transformed when people are converted to Christ and discipled, not before. In place of a demon and fortress mindset, let us ever be Jesus centered and passionate about persevering prayer.

Chapter Ten
Praying in the Face of Rejection

*"The earnest prayer of a righteous man has great power
and wonderful results."*
– James 5:16 LB

*"Hear my prayer, Oh Lord; listen to my cry!
Don't sit back unmindful of my tears."*
– Psalms 39:12 LB

I remember her well. My remembrances come from
her many manifest kindnesses to children and her potent,
passionate prayers. Mrs. Smith was one of those
intercessors who demonstrated great grace in the midst of
trial and remained unrelenting in pursuit of an answer
from God. Like many others before her she prayed in the
face of genuine rejection for years, and "through faith and
patience inherit[ed] what [had] been promised" (Hebrews
6:12).

Mrs. Smith loved Jesus and attended church many
years alone because her husband had no interest. For a
number of years their marriage appeared to be at least
average. Mr. Smith was a kind man and a good provider
who looked after their home and went to work regularly.

HEARD

After some years, however, he became distant and emotionally detached and seemed preoccupied, but gave no indication of what might be troubling him.

During this time, Mrs. Smith took a ten day vacation to visit relatives in another state. Mrs. Smith never imagined the nightmare awaiting her as she returned from her trip to find that her husband had been having an affair with her sister and her sister was now living in their home. Mr. Smith took Mrs. Smith to the guest room where he had moved all of her personal items and firmly announced, "This is the way things will be from now on. You can stay or go."

Mrs. Smith had begged God for her husband's salvation. Now this! Had God heard what she had requested of him through the years? She sought advice and counsel and received much, including a good amount unsolicited. Virtually everyone said she should leave her home, abandon her estranged husband, and seek a divorce at the first opportunity—all of which seemed logical from a human and scriptural standpoint.

But after protracted praying from a broken heart and deep embarrassment, Mrs. Smith determined it was God's will for her to stay in her home, act like a guest, stay sweet in spirit, and keep praying. So, for the next ten years she followed that course. Her husband did not offer her a divorce and she did not seek one.

For ten years Mrs. Smith followed this course, living in the guest room of her own home while her sister lived as her husband's mistress. Then, Mr. Smith began to develop severe headaches. Tests indicated that a highly voracious and usually fatal tumor had infected his brain.

Immediate surgery was required. Hearing the d
Mrs. Smith's sister immediately moved out of th
mumbling that she "was not going to play nursem
vegetable."

Shortly after the surgery was performed, Mrs.
went to visit her estranged husband. As she walked
the room, she heard the words she had been waitin
hear for years upon years. "I have seen Jesus," he s
"and he is real. He has forgiven my terrible sins." He t
asked his wife to forgive him also. Mr. Smith's surgery w
successful and he made a full recovery. Over the next fe
months their marriage was restored. With considerab
help from their pastors, they were able to rebuild thei
severely damaged relationship. In the years that followed
they served God together until both passed away from
natural causes.

Could you walk victoriously while living in such
circumstances? Could you keep your anger and broken
heart in check to the point that weeping prayer could still
be made for an unfaithful spouse? Could you have stayed
the course until a breakthrough came?

Could you respond like Mrs. Smith were you in her
place?

In Luke 18:1-8 we find an example of another
woman being rejected and the positive outcome of her
persistence.

Now he was telling them a parable to show that at all
times they ought to pray and not lose heart saying, "There
was in a certain city a judge who did not fear God and did
not respect man. And there was a widow in that city. And
she kept coming to him saying, 'Give me legal protection

from my opponent.' And for a while he was unwilling; but afterward he said to himself, 'Even though I do not fear God nor respect man, yet because this widow bothers me, I will give her legal protection, lest by her continually coming she wear me out.' And the Lord said, 'Hear what the unjust judge said; now shall not God bring about justice for his elect and those who cry to him day and night, and will he delay long over them? I tell you that he will bring about justice for them speedily. However, when the Son of Man comes, will he find faith on the earth?'"

The wife who seemed to be rejected was not rejected at all. God was watching her actions and listening to her prayers. She could truly testify to the fact that "weeping may last for the night, but a shout of joy comes in the morning" (Psalms 30:5).

A praying woman who will not quit praying until she receives an answer is a true intercessor indeed. The widow of Luke 18 triumphed over one of prayer's highest obstacles and most frequent enemies– the sense of abandonment and rejection. Mrs. Smith stood for ten years in the foothills of that mountain. The story of Mrs. Smith and the widow of Luke 18 can help you secure victory as well. For Jesus' sake, and the sake of the people for whom you are praying, don't quit too soon! Your answer is just around the corner.

Jesus said, "At all times, they ought to pray" (Luke 18:1). That is a high standard. How can we pray at all times? Is it impossible to follow the example established by Jesus himself? God does not place lofty standards in the Bible to which we cannot ascend. Obviously, Jesus

would not have included such a standard in Scripture if fulfilling it were impossible.

This same principle is taught by Paul in 1 Thessalonians 5:15-17 where he says:

"Do not repay evil for evil" (verse 15).

"Rejoice always" (verse 16).

"Pray without ceasing" (verse 17).

These are the conditions and the above is the pathway to unceasing prayer. Does this sound challenging to you? It is! Jesus knew it was, so he told his followers not to lose heart (see Luke 18:1). When your emotions perceive rejection and resistance at the point of prayer, do not be discouraged or succumb to a heavy heart and depression. Instead, do as Jesus instructed and focus your heart on rejoicing. He hears you!

Long Term Prayer

The words of Jesus keep recycling through my spirit. Men ought to pray "at all times." At all times! Pray continually! Keep praying even when you hear nothing, and feel nothing, and see nothing in response.

The unnamed but passionate and persistent widow of Luke 18 is Jesus' example to us of persistent, long term praying. Through it, we see the value of asking God for his help continually and determinedly until we receive our answer.

Like all of us, this widow had a need that could only be met through a higher power. The widow had an enemy so severe the Bible refers to him as an opponent that she needed protection from. Also, like us, the widow had a higher power available which could help her.

Unlike us, the widow's higher power, the city's judge, did not want to help her. In her day, the needs of widows were not taken seriously (even in the church, See Acts 6:1-ff). And this judge was no exception. In fact, the Bible says he did not fear God or respect man and he was unrighteous. This condition explains his cold, neglectful response to the widow and his lack of human esteem. Although she asked for his help time after time after time, the judge ignored this desperate woman and her opponent went unfairly unchecked.

Have you ever felt what the widow inevitably felt? Have you felt absolutely alone in your prayer times? Have your circumstances screamed back at you when no immediate answer to prayer arrived at the time you needed it? Have you ever thought or said, "No one really understands or cares, and there is probably no help for my situation"?

Because the judge wouldn't help her, the power of the law was out of force. But the widow did not give up. She just kept asking and asking and asking until she received the answer she longed for. And we should do the same.

Many Christians envision our higher power, God Himself, as a judge. Thanks be to God, he is not like the judge in Luke 18! In fact, God cares so much for us that he bends down from heaven just to hear our prayers (Psalms 116:2 NLT). The Bible says that he ALWAYS hears us (John 1:42 NLT). He instructs us to pray all the time. And if we ask, and keep on asking, like the widow, we too will obtain answers to our needs (Matthew 7:7 NIV).

The parable shows the true condition of the world system then and now and its inherent inability to deliver answers into life's dilemmas. How can a believer expect to secure lasting help in a flawed fallen culture? Nothing in the world system—be it wealth, power, or material goods—can provide for our spiritual needs. How can a believer expect to secure lasting help in a flawed and fallen culture?

It's simple: continual, long term, persistent prayer. When the widow was consistently asking for help from the judge, the world's system provided her with rebuff and resistance. It will do the same for you. It is in such seasons of delay, in times or perceived rejection, that the heart must go on deep into the resources of God. When you have nothing else to hold on to but his Word, keep asking. It will not fail you. Your character will grow in this environment. The emotions may rail against the spirit, but patience will bear fruit.

We must learn the discipline of consistent, ongoing prayer when our much needed answer is not available!

The Good Attitude of the Heart

Someone has said, "The attitude of the heart sets one's altitude." This means that if we believe, and if our beliefs are reflected in our actions, we will eventually receive the response we desire from God. Our widow from Luke 18 was resolute. When she didn't get an answer from the judge, she did not go around complaining and discouraged. Instead she stood immovable on the premise that legal protection was her right. Based on this belief, she "kept coming to him." How do you drive away discouragement when real, in-your-face circumstances all around have set themselves against your requests? You stand immovable in the knowledge that you have the right to come boldly before his throne of grace. This assurance will sustain you and keep your heart attitude positive.

Oh, the mystery of the heart, the complex unknowable heart. Jesus said not to be discouraged even though it looks like you are being rejected, your enemies are prospering, and heaven does not respond. Keep on praying and maintaining a positive attitude. How can you do that? *Focus on the character of God!*

That is precisely what Abraham did when God asked for his son as a sacrifice. He already said to his servants, "I and the boy [will] go over there. We will worship and then *we* will come back to you" (Genesis 22:5 NIV, emphasis added). How could Abraham be sure *both* of them would return? Abraham knew and trusted God's character. Because of his attitude, God called him his friend. Job trusted in God's character in his darkest hour. He said, "I know that my Redeemer lives, and in the end will stand upon the earth...yet in my flesh I shall see God...though my heart yearns within me" (Job 19:25-27 NIV). God rewarded his attitude by giving him double of everything that was taken from him. James 5:11 explains how God relates to us in seasons of unrequited prayer: "Behold we count those blessed who endured. You have heard of the endurance of Job and seen the outcome of the Lord's dealing, that the Lord is full of compassion and merciful". When persisting in prayer, we must do like Abraham and

Job. Keep your eyes on the character of God and let that raise your heart attitude into the heavens.

The Timing of Answers to Prayer

For reasons that God alone knows and controls, there are often delays–at times, long ones–in receiving answers to prayer. There are delays when you "legally" have a right to an answer and delays when all human conditions have been met, and even delays when the motive is correct and the request is clearly within the will of God. We should remember, however, that the will of God involves timing and a fixed point when he chooses to answer.

Delayed answers are especially troublesome when you have an active opponent. This opponent may or may not be another person. It can be a troublesome situation you are facing, a decision to be made, or perhaps an incurable disease. How long can you wait, then, for an answer? Habakkuk knew the pressure of the delay problem when he was constrained in Jerusalem surrounded by hostile Chaldeans. He received no rapid response from God when he cried out, "How long, o Lord, will I call for help, and Thou wilt not hear? I cry unto Thee, 'Violence'. Yet Thou dost not save" (Habakkuk 1:2).

Two verses later the same prophet said, "Therefore the law is ignored and justice is never upheld, for the wicked surround the righteous; therefore, justice comes out perverted" (Habakkuk 1:4).

Just as Habakkuk was delayed by perverted justice, sometimes the answers to prayer are delayed by the nature the sources from which we hope to receive a response. Sometimes these sources are fundamentally flawed and, in some cases, unrighteous. We will not receive any *supernatural* help from denominational relationships, counsel, the advice of friends, self-help books, or prominent ministries. These will produce only short term help. Nothing generated from fleshly, earth-bound sources will bring supernatural answers to prayer.

Our widow's parable does not end in failure or unanswered requests. Her answer was delayed, but ultimately she was answered. Remember the unjust judge's words in Luke 18:5? He said, "This bothers me". That is, she kept coming and asking and seeking and knocking. She was always in his face. He had two options: either answer her and give her protection, or listen to her request over and over again. She was not going away. He did not respect her, care about her need, or regard God. But he did care about his personal comfort, however, and knew this widow was relentless in her pursuit of justice. While his response was driven in self interest, the widow got what she wanted and needed by persevering.

God is far different in both character and kindness than the earthly judge who indifferently delayed and deferred. In Luke 18:8 we see the grace of God at work when it says, "He will bring about justice for them [His elect] speedily." The word "speedily" does not mean God will hurry. Rather, it means that when the time comes for him to answer, the answer will be released suddenly. The term is similar to the one used by John in Revelation 22:12 (KJV) when he quotes Jesus saying, "Behold I come quickly." Hurrying is not intended or implied. Suddenness is! Prayer can be made for a person, circumstance, illness, or problems for years and years without a visible response –or at least one we understand. Then, in what seems to be an instant, he answers!

A young missionary reported that the spiritual climate in the country where he worked had "suddenly" changed. In prior years, public evangelistic meetings would draw only ten or fifteen people. Today crowds number in the thousands. What brought about that change? Over seventy years of intercession was being answered. Remember, with regard to answering prayer, *God has eternity in mind, not our wants and wishes.* Hebrews 6:12 tells us that we obtain his promises 'by faith and patience.'

Faith and patience! These are terms that expose our character before they touch our needs. Faith is the attitude of belief towards God; patience is the heart attitude that accepts long-suffering and quiet waiting. Faith and gratitude-filled waiting are keys to getting answers from God which always come in his perfect timing.

Intercession and the Growth of Faith

"When the Son of Man comes, will he find faith on the earth" (Luke 18:8 NASV)? What is the linkage between intercession and the growth of faith? One of the more mature phases of prayer is the prayer for wisdom. The Lord taught his disciples to pray, "Thy kingdom come... on earth as it is in heaven" (Matthew 6:10 NASV). There is something to be gained by that which is known. Intense intercession will access a small amount of God's knowledge about the matters in our prayers. When we know what God wants, we can pray for the goals he has revealed and cooperate with him in bringing them to pass. Those who *pray* well also *see* well and the *seeing* produces specific intercessions. Faith is linked to prayer and intercession in the realm of insight into divine secrets and, when based on revealed information, faith is launched heavenward.

Faith has two environments in which it grows well. First, it grows by reading and hearing God's word through preaching, music, tapes, and books. Secondly, faith is nurtured in effective intercession which increases our ability to exercise faith and belief that God will answer. Intercession is a place of revelation. I will say it boldly: the people with the greatest expression of genuine faith are also persistent, long-term intercessors.

Remember Mrs. Smith from the beginning of this chapter? Her persistence in prayer is a real life example of our Luke 18 widow. They both persisted in intercession. Mrs. Smith prayed ten years, kept a good attitude, stayed faithful to God, and hooked her faith to the character and Word of God. The wonderful ending is this, God answered! The widow's story is a tremendous encouragement to persist and not to quit too soon. God's timing, character, eternal purposes and faith expansion are all at work even though he may seem distant and our prayers dead. *He is there and He will respond.*

Chapter Eleven
Tears, Weeping and Prayer

"There is a time to weep."
– Ecclesiastics 3:4

"Let your tears come, let them water your soul."
– Eileen Mayhew

"Tears are often the telescope by which men see far into heaven."
– Henry Ward Beecher

"They that sow in tears shall reap in joy."
– Psalm 126:5

    Some close personal friends reported an unusual event that happened as part of a large prayer gathering. The speaker of the evening called ten pastors to the front of the church. Each of them were asked to read one of the ten commandments from Exodus and, after reading, lead the entire audience in a prayer of repentance for violating that law of God. All ten followed the directions given. At the end of the service, the speaker uttered an extremely solemn summary. He said, "There were no tears, no passion. Because there were no tears, there will be no spiritual rain in this city for a long time to come because none of you shed any tears." There had been little weeping, few tears, no overt demonstrations of passion during the entire prayer event. Even the repentance over breaking God's laws had been a rather academic, cerebral exercise.

This dramatic public exposure highlights a significant issue related to the quality of prayer. *In prayer services, one sees few tears these days!* I have personally attended dozens of prayer events that were dry. Is that your experience as well? Could it be that most prayer services offer God little more than cognitive blips that vibrate the ears of the hearers but have no power and cause no reaction in hell or response in heaven? When have you been in a prayer meeting that was filled with weeping petitioners? Most people just don't easily weep. The conditions in which and with which we live are not yet appalling enough, not heartbreaking enough, not yet galling enough to be challenged by weeping saints. Cold hearts are manifested by dry eyes.

There are critics, of course, who would say weeping, teary prayers are just not needed. They might even say that type of behavior is for the emotional fringe types. Both the Bible and the historical record of God's church show the value that he places on those who weep and the need to be contrite in heart.

The Old Testament prophet Jeremiah is known as the weeping prophet. Look at what he said on one occasion when Israel was being threatened with attack and captivity.

"But if you will not listen to it

My soul will sob in secret for such pride;

And my eyes will bitterly weep

And flow down with tears,

Because the flock of the Lord has been taken captive."

– Jeremiah 13:17

Can you feel Jeremiah's heart in these words? He is expressing deep grief over Israel's condition. The nation was in great peril and in danger of becoming captive to a hostile power. How could he, as a prophet and man of God, stand idly by and allow his nation, the chosen people of God, to slide into a political and spiritual abyss without crying out to God? He had to weep and cry out to God in desperation and so must we. Elsewhere in this book we discuss Hannah's fervent prayers. One should remember notice was taken of her situation when she was asked, "Hannah, why do you weep?" (1 Samuel 1:8).

Job is one of the best known persons in the Bible who exemplifies a life filled with trials, severe trials. Chapter thirty of his book is one in which he bemoans his humiliating state and condition. At such times, when circumstances are especially difficult, there is little more to do than weep. Words often cannot fully express the complete sentiment of the soul. Tears, somehow, in ways we don't fully understand, act as a relief mechanism.

Consider these verses from Job, chapter 30:

"And now my soul is poured out with me,

days of affliction have seized me." (v.16)

"At night it pierced my bones within me

And my gnawing pains take no rest." (v.17)

"Have I not wept for the one whose life is hard

Was not my soul grieved for the needy?" (v.25)

"Therefore my harp is turned to mourning

And my flute to the sound of those who weep." (v.31)

Can you feel the weight and distress on Job's heart? Every word is laden with passion. When I review the words above I am taken into his pathos and pain.

Jeremiah, Isaiah, Job, and many others wept! And through their weeping, God responded to them. What is it in our souls or minds that keeps us from weeping? Why are so many prayers dry or tearless?

Weeping contrition also can be a corporate matter, a group exercise if you will. Israel wept as a nation when they were in danger of a military attack from the Ammonites. The Ammonites were threatening Israel with horrible destruction. They had sent word ahead that they were coming, and would disgrace Israel by gouging out the right eye of every citizen of Jabesh Gilead. The story is told in 1 Samuel 11:1-15:

"The people wept (v.4)

[Saul posed the question] What is the matter with the people that they weep?" (v.5)

Corporate weeping is an appropriate response to danger. Can we correctly say believers are under spiritual attacks these days? If so, would tear soaked intercession be an appropriate response in the light of current world conditions? Do things like the brutal death and destruction visited upon New York City, electrical blackouts that affected 50 million people in the USA and entire nations in Europe, AIDS, radical religionists of various ilks trying to reshape the world, financial instability, millions dying of hunger and various diseases– do any of these or any combination of these move your heart? There are many reasons to weep today. Do you?

In the Bible there are many reasons to weep in contrition and prayer. Here are some:

- Abraham weeping over the *death* of Sarah (Genesis 23:2).

- The people of Israel weeping in *complaint* over the diet on the exodus (Genesis 16:2, 3, 8).

- Joseph weeping over his *estrangement* from his brothers (Genesis 44:30).

- David and his people wept over the *attack* of the Amalekites. (I Samuel 30:1).

- David wept over the *death* of his child. (2 Samuel 12:16).

- King of Judah as he turned to God when facing *impending judgment* (2 Chronicles 34:27).

- When Ezra read the law during the *restoration* of Jerusalem (Nehemiah 8:9-12).

- When Isaiah promised *God's answer* to the people's cry (Isaiah 30:19).

- Because of a *broken heart* (Lamentations 1:16).

- Weeping is to be the activity of the priests. (Joel 2:17).

- As an expression of one's heart motives (Luke 6:21).

- Early Christians over Paul's prophesied imprisonment (Acts 21:7-13).

- As an act of contrition and humility (James 4:8-9).

- As a predecessor to judgment (James 5:1).

- The women at the tomb of Jesus *(death)* (John 20:13-15).

- Response to rejection and judgement for disobedience (Matthew 8:12, 22:13, 24:5 1, 25:30).

Some Things to Ponder Concerning Tears

There are some mysteries about weeping, and characteristics to reflect on concerning tears. What do verses like these mean? "My tears have been my meat night and day" (Psalm 42:3). Or "Thou hast fed them with the bread of tears, and thou hast made them to drink tears in large measure" (Psalm 80:5 NASV). Does weeping and tear shedding feed our spiritual person in some mystical but profoundly important ways?

Revelation 5:8 speaks about "golden bowls full of incense which are the prayers of the saints." Some translations call these heavenly containers "bowls." We don't have a full understanding at the moment about what all that means, what is implied, and what is to be revealed about the "bowls." Could it be David had a distant view when he said, "Put thou my tears in a bottle" (Psalm

56:12)? Could he be talking about Revelation 5:8? If so, what does it mean? At the least, it means God takes notice of weeping and tears and that they, the tears, are not lost. The tears have value to him.

Finally, there is this great promise for those who weep. "They that sow in tears shall reap in joy" (Psalm 126:5). Weeping is seasonal. There is a time when it is required and needed. But that season will be followed by another called joy. What wonderful solace is found in the words of an old southern spiritual song I heard once, "We can't weep always because morning draws nigh." No matter how grim your circumstance, how bereft of hope and stripped of visible potential your life may be at the moment, cry out to him. He will turn your valley of *"baca,"* the place of weeping, into a place of refreshing.

Practical Matters

As a culture, Americans don't cry easily. Men, in particular, have been culturally formed by being told "men don't cry" or, if found crying, "get up boy, stop that crying and act like a man." That wrong counsel sets a negative value on tears from a young age as far as males are concerned. Rarely are men seen crying in public because of the perceived weakness of that emotional expression. We bring that cultural value to church. When we approach God we try to do it in our own strength. Therefore, few weep before him.

There are additional issues as well. Heart hardness, unconfessed sin, local church ethos or atmosphere (casual is cool), peer pressure, the "success gospel" which in its lifetime has never uttered a word about contrition–all work directly against brokenness and weeping before God. We should be frontally reminded that God is "near to the broken hearted and those of a contrite spirit." If we draw near to God with a heart of passion for him and some tears in our eyes birthed from that passion, I am biblically, experientially, and personally convinced that God will respond! There is a "time to weep." Could it be now?

Chapter Twelve
When God is Silent

Songs come and go in popularity. That is as true of Christian songs, even hymns, as of any other type of music. In worship, one generation might perk up and sing one of "their" songs with gusto while the younger (or older folks) roll their eyes and shrug. Arguing about favorite worship songs rarely does anything but pit generations against each other.

"In the Garden" is one of those songs. Today's senior citizens love it, sing it from memory and request it in worship services or sing-a-longs. Most people under about fifty years old don't care for it, musically or lyrically. The song was written by Charles Austin Miles, a book editor and aspiring musician, in 1912. The song wasn't written in a garden: one morning Miles was doing his devotions in his cold, dreary, windowless basement in New Jersey. The passage that day was the story of Mary meeting the risen Jesus outside the garden tomb. Inspired by the image, the song came together quickly. The Billy Sunday evangelistic crusade popularized the song, playing it in its meetings around the country. In the 1950s country singers Roy Rogers and Dale Evans recorded the song, as did pop crooner Perry Como. Christians who grew up in that era are fond of its style and content, and it probably brings

back happy memories for them.

Maybe "In the Garden" suits your taste in music and maybe it doesn't. Regardless, the song is interesting because of how it portrays Christian prayer:

I come to the garden alone
While the dew is still on the roses
And the voice I hear falling on my ear
The Son of God discloses.

Refrain

And He walks with me, and He talks with me,
And He tells me I am His own;
And the joy we share as we tarry there,
None other has ever known.

He speaks, and the sound of His voice,
Is so sweet the birds hush their singing,
And the melody that He gave to me
Within my heart is ringing.

Refrain

I'd stay in the garden with Him
Though the night around me be falling,
But He bids me go; through the voice of woe
His voice to me is calling.

It's a beautiful image of what Christian prayer is like. Or is it what prayer is like *sometimes?* Or what prayer is *supposed* to be like? Or what we wish that it *could* be?

Truthfully, sometimes prayer is like that. But, just as truthfully, sometimes it's not. Sometimes it's hard to bring ourselves to pray, and when we do muster the energy, the praying itself is hard. Sometimes, it feels like you've arrived in the garden and just waited, but God didn't show. You don't hear the sweet voice that hushes the birds or embeds a melody in your heart. It's as if God has "stood you up" on your garden date.

All Christians have experienced times when God seems silent. It's as if our prayers were falling on deaf ears, or onto no ears at all. Sometimes prayer feels like it does when you're talking to someone on the phone, telling them a long story, and it occurs to you that you haven't heard any response from them in a while. You ask, "Are you still there?" You look at your phone and realize that the call disconnected five minutes ago and you've been rambling on to a dead line.

Other times, prayer can feel like waiting for an important phone call, or email, or letter. You stare at the phone, check the line, call yourself. You check your email over and over, maybe send yourself a test email from another account to make sure it's still working. You stare down the street, waiting for the letter carrier. But no matter how much you check or how anxious you get, the sought-after communication doesn't come.

Sometimes prayer can make you feel silly when it becomes coupled with doubt. You pray, read some scripture, pray some more. You sit quietly, put on devotional music, lie prostrate on your floor. But no matter what you do, or how hard you try, all you hear is the clock ticking and the neighbor's lawn mower. You wonder what's for dinner. There is no breakthrough, no secret garden, no sweet voice falling on your ear.

Other times, prayer can feel like you are lost and no one will give you directions. Or it feels like you have to assemble some piece of equipment without the instructions. Or it feels like you have a boss that won't just tell you what they want you to do. You ask God how to handle some problem, or which alternative he wants you to choose, and get no answer.

Sometimes prayer doesn't feel like a dew-covered garden, but like an arid wasteland. You feel thirsty, depleted, lethargic, bored. Sometimes it feels like a chore. Sometimes prayer can feel like an awkward dinner party, with you sitting at the other end of the table from a stern and silent patriarch, picking at your food and wondering if you can skip dessert and get away quickly.

Sometimes prayer can feel like a marriage with "issues." When asked about their day, both spouses say, "Fine," and then watch TV in silence for the rest of the evening.

Silence *can* be a sweet thing, and silence with God can be some of the sweetest moments in our lives. But if we are honest we have to admit that there are moments in the Christian life where prayer is simply difficult. The hardest of these moments are when God seems silent: not the good kind of silent, but a painful and strained emptiness that can cast our very faith into doubt. These can be the most lonely and devastating moments of our lives.

Can Christians, filled with the Holy Spirit, ever fail to hear God's voice? Of course we believe that God never abandons us, and the Holy Spirit never leaves us. God never stops speaking with us, and the Holy Spirit never stops speaking for us.

Yet there are times, even to the most mature Christians, when God *seems* silent. Even famous Christians, heroes of the faith who have done great acts of mercy, written books, led movements, built churches and evangelized nations, have had seasons in their lives when God seemed quiet and far away. In an earlier chapter we described the intimacy Mother Teresa sometimes felt with God: like an old, married couple sitting on a porch, saying nothing. But after Mother Teresa died in 1997 a number of her private letters were released. In some, written to her spiritual mentors, confessors and friends, she revealed that she had lived through periods when God had seemed so silent that at times she doubted his existence. There were seasons in her life when, in her own words, "she felt no presence of God whatsoever." These times of divine quiet, when prayers echoed back like shouts in a canyon, were emotionally devastating. She wrote, "Where is my faith? Even deep down ... there is nothing but emptiness and darkness ... If there be God–please forgive me. When I try to raise my thoughts to Heaven, there is such convicting emptiness that those very thoughts return like sharp knives and hurt my very soul...How painful is this unknown pain–I have no Faith. Repulsed, empty, no faith, no love, no zeal...what do I labor for?"

In 1678 John Bunyan wrote one of the classic descriptions of the joys and trials of the Christian life, *The Pilgrim's Progress*. Written as an allegorical novel, it follows the adventures of the lead character, Christian, as he travels from his home in the City of Destruction to the Celestial City (Heaven). Christian, equipped with the full armor of God, defeats enemies and resists temptations. About three-quarters of the way through the story, after Christian is no longer a new believer and has seen great evidence of God's power, he comes to a castle occupied by a giant named Despair. Christian briefly trespasses on the giant's estate, and thus is captured and tossed into the castle dungeon. The name of the place is Doubting Castle, and Christian is severely beaten by Despair. He lies in the dungeon, bruised and bloody, sighing and moaning in pain. He loses hope of ever getting out of the place. Despair tries to persuade Christian to commit suicide, as his only way of escaping Doubting Castle. He is saved by remembering that earlier in the story that he had been given a key called Promise, that was supposed to be able to open any door. Christian tries it on the dungeon door, and thus is able to escape Despair and Doubting Castle.

This incident from *Pilgrim's Progress* reminds us that times of silence, despair and doubt are not only *possible* in the Christian life, they are to be periodically expected. The mature Christian may not be able to avoid them, but he can be prepared to endure them.

But why do we have times when God seems silent? There are many reasons, and for any one of us there may be more than one reason during a given season of our prayer life.

One reason is "ambient noise." Imagine that you are talking with a friend. A normal, conversational speaking tone is about sixty decibels. In a quiet place (like a private room, or a dew-covered garden) we can hear each other clearly because the background (ambient) noise is about ten or twenty decibels. Our friend's voice is at least forty decibels louder than that. But imagine we are having our conversation not in a private garden, but on a busy street corner. City traffic is about eighty decibels, twenty *louder* than our friend's voice. Our friend has to speak up to be heard over the ambient noise, or we have to listen very carefully. The same thing can happen in our prayer life. God may only seem silent because the rest of our life is too loud; all the other voices, distractions, stresses and thoughts running through our mind drown him out. God might be speaking, but we might not be able to hear him until we turn down the volume on everything competing with his voice.

Sometimes God seems silent because the conversation is moving on his timetable, not ours. Every conversation has a pace, a rhythm. If our prayers are an ongoing conversation with God, what makes us think that it will be at our pace? What if what we think is silence is really just a pause? Perhaps God just spoke to us recently, and is giving us time to digest what he just said before he continues. Perhaps he is waiting for us to reply. All of us have sent a letter, or an email, and waited anxiously for a reply. Days go by and as we stare at our empty mailbox we begin to doubt that the other person is going to reply at all. Sometimes, when the reply does come, we get an explanation as to why it took so long, but sometimes we do not.

There's another reason why God can seem silent, and it's rooted in an old saying: "It's darkest under the lighthouse." When we are young believers, approaching God for the first time, we can be flattered by all the attention God seems to lavish on us. Every experience in the Kingdom seems new and delicious. As we mature (get closer to the lighthouse) our faith becomes less about us.

We become attuned to the work of the Kingdom. We care for the sick in Calcutta, or work to bring the Gospel to the Middle East. It seems that our conversations with God are all about other people and other issues. Sometimes, we miss the conversations God used to have about us and our concerns. When that happens, God can seem silent to us. In reality, he may be waiting for us to be less self-absorbed and to care about what he cares about.

Sometimes God *has* spoken, but is waiting for us to act on what he said. Maybe he gave clear instructions, and we haven't paid attention or are deliberately ignoring them. Perhaps he wants us to obey the last thing he told us to do before he gives us any new direction.

Another reason God might seem silent is that he's forcing us to grow up. St. John of the Cross was a sixteenth century Spanish monk who wrote *Dark Night of the Soul*, one of the most influential works on spiritual growth and prayer in Church history. Since then, "dark night of the soul" is used to describe a season of spiritual loneliness when God seems distant and silent. In his commentary on his original work, St. John wrote, "The soul, after it has been definitely converted to the service of God, is, as a rule, spiritually nurtured and caressed by God, even as is the tender child by its loving mother, who warms it with the heat of her bosom and nurtures it with sweet milk and soft and pleasant food, and carries it and caresses it in her arms." In other words, God gives the new Christian the sort of attention that a mother gives a new baby. Our prayer lives feel intimate and vibrant. God holds us close and speaks soothingly and often.

St. John went on, arguing that God is not content to let us remain spiritual infants forever. He wants us to mature, to develop discipline, strength and wisdom. "But as the child grows bigger, the mother gradually ceases caressing it, and, hiding her tender love, puts bitter aloes upon her sweet breast, sets down the child from her arms and makes it walk upon its feet, so that it may lose the habits of a child and betake itself to more important and substantial occupations." God sometimes allows us to go through the dark night of the soul so that we can learn to not be afraid of the dark.

Even if God *seems* to be silent at times in our prayer life, we know that he never truly is silent. We know that he continues to speak to us through his written Word the Bible, through the movement of the Spirit in the Church, and through the wise counsel of godly believers. We know that even when he seems quiet, and our prayers feel empty and dry, the problem is often that we aren't listening, or don't have the patience to hear him.

But like Christian, languishing in the dungeon of the giant Despair's Doubting Castle, we have a key: the promises of God. He promises us that he will not abandon us, that he is with us always, to the very end of the age. And he promises us that he will send us the Counselor, his Holy Spirit, to be with us to the end of the age.

As others have said through the ages, I believe in the sun even when it isn't shining. I believe in love even when I do not feel it. And I believe in God even when he is silent.

Chapter Thirteen
The Reception Room of Prayer

*"And because you answer prayer, all mankind will come
to you with their requests."*
– Psalms 65:2 LB

"Seek those things which are above."
– Colossians 3:1 KJV

*"Oh Jehovah, God of my salvation, I have wept before
you day and night.*
Now hear my prayers; oh, listen to my cry."
– Psalms 88:1-2 LB

Prayer is often an awkward exercise. To a
sophisticated person, it seems genuinely ludicrous to
speak into the air as though speaking to someone near,
when no one is visible. Yet adherents to many different
religions practice something they call prayer.

For Christians, prayer is neither ludicrous nor futile.
Those who believe in Jesus Christ also believe his word
that he will not and cannot lie. Christians accept the
proposition that if God is sought after by means of prayer–

in whatever form, volume or emotional state–it is on the basis that there is a benevolent God in heaven who can hear and who will respond. So often the human side of making needs known to God seems like a lifeless, lackluster, intellectually-challenging enterprise. In reality, it is everything but that.

The purpose of this chapter is to investigate the heavenly side of the prayer equation. Where do my prayers go? What happens to them when they arrive where they are going? What happens in the interim between a prayer prayed and a prayer answered? What actions take place at the Father's throne as a response and consequence of prayer?

At the beginning of Revelation 4, the point of view moves from earth to heaven, from exhortations to the churches in Asia to a specific focus on God's throne. Verses 1 and 2 state, "Come up here, and I will show you what must take place after these things. Immediately I was in the Spirit, and behold, a throne was standing in heaven and one was sitting on the throne." This is what we must see–the throne of God with God upon it! That is where our prayers find hearing and response.

Chapters four and five of Revelation are a special segment in a much larger prophetic drama. The focus is in heaven and on God's throne. The throne scene comes immediately prior to the cataclysmic outpouring of judgment. At the beginning of chapter 6, judgment begins. The activities in chapter five are full of consolation and hope since they describe what God is doing on his throne and how the angels and elders are helping him administrate his kingdom. He is concerned with intercession. Prayer is always before him.

Revelation 5:8 says, "And when he had taken the book, the four living creatures and the twenty-four elders fell before the Lamb, having each one a harp, and the golden bowls full of incense, which are the prayers of the saints." Who are these personalities around the throne of God? According to Revelation 5:11, there are millions of angels there. John uses the word "myriads" which means countless, impossible to number, or, said plainly, millions of angels.

In verse eight, the four living creatures represent all living things on, under, and over the earth. The twenty-four elders represent the twelve tribes of Israel and the twelve apostles of the Lamb. However, the centerpiece and the greatest personality of all in the throne room is Father God seated upon his throne. Since God is the center, we must pay attention to the things that concern him. Whatever draws God's attention must also capture our full attention and become the things to which we commit our time and energy.

Remember, Revelation 5 shows God on his throne. Revelation 6 starts horrific judgement on the earth. Therefore, God on his throne is concerned with pre-judgment matters. His concerns, focused in the life of his people, are just two. He is concerned with praise and prayer. Here we are concerned only with the latter, prayer. But praise must be interjected briefly since praise touches prayer. In our key verse above, we see that each elder was given a harp, which is often shown in the Scriptures as an instrument of worship: "Praise the Lord with the harp"; Sing unto the Lord with the harp"; "Praise him with the psaltery and harp"(Psalms 33:2, 98:5, 150:3 KJV). Therefore we see that worship is primary at the throne of

Ascension ministries

Ascension Anointing

God and it also has a specific kinship to prayer. Both worship and intercession are ascension ministries; that is, their focus is always upwards towards God.

Praise is the gate opener for prayer. Psalms 100:4 (KJV) says, "Enter into his gates with thanksgiving, and into his courts with praise" and in Revelation 5:1 4 (KJV) we see that the "elders fell down and worshipped him."

In many church cultures, praise times and prayer times are separated. However, praise and prayer are two expressions of the same ascension anointing. Both are designed to send something upward into God's presence. Both go from earth to heaven. Both require individuals to exercise their will positively towards God. Both need the assistance of the Holy Spirit to bring a living dynamic into them. Otherwise, they, like many religious things, become nothing more than clanging cymbals and empty forms.

Perhaps as the body of Christ matures, our praising and praying will be actively engaged simultaneously. Once we fully understand kingdom dynamics, we will be able to move freely between intimate high praise and groaning intercession. Why do we have a prayer meeting at one time and a worship event at another? Why should they be separated here? After all, they are fully mingled at the throne of God.

God places high value on those who pray and on their prayers. Some of the personalities nearest to God himself have been given the task of receiving, recording, sustaining, and safely keeping the prayers of the saints. He has planned for prayer to reach him and to be safely kept till the hour of response.

The elders of the throne room have been given

golden containers called censers or "odors", an Old Testament term for a perfume container. This container has the characteristic of holding precious liquid and releasing its aroma at the same time. Exodus 25:6, 30:8, 31:11, and 37:29 speak of the "spices for the anointing oil and for the fragrant incense," "perpetual incense before the Lord," "fragrant incense for the holy place," and the "pure, fragrant incense of spices." Incense is that which can be turned into fragrance by fire. King David said, "[May] my prayer be counted as incense" (Psalms 141:2).

In relationship to prayer, incense has two characteristics. First, the smoke goes upward just as prayer goes Godward from the heart. Second, the aroma goes outward to cover the smell of the slaughtered animals and burning flesh with sweetness. No matter how hot the trials of life may be, prayer, like incense, brings sweetness like nothing else can. It changes the atmosphere. It is perfume to God. He likes it!

God loves prayer, and prayer has his attention. In Revelation 8 terrible judgements hurl towards the earth. Yet, in the midst, intercessors are consoled by the fact that their prayers remain before his throne. We see in verses 3 and 4 that:

Another angel came and stood at the altar, holding a golden censer, and much incense was given to him that he might add it to the prayers of all the saints upon the golden altar which was before the throne. And the smoke of the incense, with prayers of the saints, went up before God out of the angel's hand.

Here again, are those two components, praise and prayer, linked together.

Even in the midst of Revelation judgement, God was mindful and merciful and valued the things said to him. It is critically important to remember that all the prayers of all the saints of all the ages are *simultaneously* before God. The prayers at the throne include all those accumulated from all the saints of all the ages, plus those arriving moment by moment. Is it not comforting to know that your prayers are mingled with the prayers of people such as Moses, Elijah, John the Baptist, and the apostle Paul?

Followers of God should be rightly encouraged by the scenery of the throne room and the activities there as they relate to prayer. Since our prayers go the Father's throne, they have a future. They are active and do not diminish in power, influence or potential. Once at the Father's throne, they are tended to by the throne room staff. What a comforting thought that *the Father's throne is the reception room for our prayers.*

Let us, for a moment, bring our gaze back to earth to visit a praying man and inquire about his prayer experiences. As a background, let's look in the Old Testament at Daniel chapters 9 and 10. Daniel's position in prayer brought him to this commitment: "I gave my attention to the Lord God to seek him by prayer and supplications, with fasting, sackcloth, and ashes" (Daniel 9:3). Daniel lived under a prophetic anointing in the sense that he was able to predict the future course of nations, yet he and his people were in captivity.

Daniel 9 is overwhelmingly prophetic in nature. To fully understand the chapter and glean the prayer principle, we must carefully examine Daniel's prayer posture and God's response to it. It was Daniel's praying that released prophetic information about the nations of the world and opened heaven just a crack so the chemistry by which prayer functions can be seen.

> *"Now while I was speaking and praying and confessing my sin and the sin of my people Israel, and presenting my supplication before the Lord on behalf of the holy mountain of my God, while I was still speaking in prayer, then the man Gabriel, whom I had seen in the vision previously, came to me in my extreme weariness about the time of the evening offering. And he gave me instruction and talked with me, and said, "O Daniel, I have now come forth to give you insight with understanding. At the beginning of your supplications the command was issued, and I have come to you, for you are highly esteemed; give heed to the message and gain understanding of the vision."*

– Daniel 9:20-23

Daniel's prayer was for understanding. He had prayed almost the entire day and at mid-afternoon Gabriel, one of the archangels of God, appeared to speak with him. I wonder what it would be like to get a prayer answered through an archangel? It is the request-and-answer process we must grasp and understand thoroughly. Notice the phrase from Daniel 9:23: "At the beginning of your supplication the command was issued." Place this information next to something said of Gabriel two verses earlier: "Gabriel, whom I had seen in the vision previously, being caused swiftly to fly..."

These matters seemed unrelated but, in fact, they are very much related to one another. There is urgency in the Father's heart to hear and answer prayer. God was so concerned about what Daniel was saying to him that he swiftly dispatched Gabriel, one of the most important of all the archangels, to Daniel. Said in another way, God ordered Gabriel to Daniel, *and in a hurry.*

Encouragement is to be found here by all those who wonder if God really hears and listens, and when. This Scripture is clear about the *when* of God's response. He responded when Daniel first prayed. How does this square, then, with the fact Daniel had been praying all day? Can this be correct? Does God answer immediately but we must continue for hours or days to become aware of what he intends? Based on this and another verse in Daniel 10, it is safe to say there is no interference in prayer going up to God; however, the response may be delayed because of demonic influences in the atmosphere or because of timing.

Daniel 10 records a similar incident. In this chapter Daniel had fasted and prayed twenty-one days as there was need to release more of God's power. Verse 12 explains God's response to the fast:

> *"Then he said to me, 'Do not be afraid, Daniel, for from the first day that you set your heart on understanding this and on humbling yourself before your God, your words were heard, and I have come in response to your words.'"*

In Daniel 9, the spokesperson was Gabriel. In Daniel 10 the spokesperson is Michael the mighty archangel. When Daniel began to pray, God responded by sending major help (see Hebrews 1:14). Yet it was three weeks before Daniel received an answer. Daniel 10:13 explains the delay. Demon powers, present in the air over Persia, blocked God's response. From this we see the devil has power, but not ultimate authority.

Certainly one of the messages arising from the Daniel passages is: *don't quit too soon!* If you have prayed long and hard about a matter without an answer, take consolation and know there are persons at the Father's throne assigned to receive and look after your prayers. They are on duty, twenty-four hours a day, every day, in their position next to God the Father.

You were heard and responded to by the Father the moment you prayed and *an angel is enroute to you now with your answer* (although, as we will see in the next chapter, God will allow you to receive that answer when he judges the time to be right). Meditate on these things and rejoice because you have been both heard and responded to by the Father.

Chapter Fourteen
Sowing and Reaping

"Those who sow in tears shall reap joy.
Yes, they go out weeping, carrying seed for sowing,
And return singing, carrying their sheaves."
– Psalms 126:5-6 LB

The law of sowing and reaping is a universal principle affecting every dimension of life. Do you remember the old adage, "If you want to have friends, you must show yourself friendly"? This is an example of the sowing and reaping process.

The Bible uses this same principle to explain spiritual dynamics. If we sow to the flesh, we will reap corruption; sow to the Spirit and reap eternal life (Galatians 6:8). In terms of finances, if we sow sparingly, we will reap sparingly (2 Corinthians 9:6). These are but two of many dimensions of life that function within the power and influence of the law of sowing and reaping. I use the term "law" because sowing and reaping, in any dimension, is an irrevocable, universal law. Where there is sowing, there will be reaping and harvest.

Here is how it works. Everyone has an opportunity

to invest life beyond self-interest. Philanthropy, community service and volunteerism are a few avenues in which we can invest our time and talents.

Sowing and reaping are graphically demonstrated in the botanical kingdom. For example, we plant corn seed. Add some time, warmth and moisture, and every healthy seed will produce a stalk. On that stalk will grow one to three ears of corn, each bearing hundreds of kernels. That is the principle. Plant seed, wait for a defined season, and then reap. Let me express this principle another way. One always reaps the same thing sown, always reaps later, and always reaps more. That is, one corn seed planted results in hundreds reaped.

Can this principle of sowing and reaping also apply to prayer and intercession? Powerfully so! In the corn illustration, it is possible to sow one small seed and reap hundreds more in return. It is also possible to pray one small Spirit-filled and God led prayer and change a nation. Remember Elijah and his little cloud?

Every historical revival has been preceded by long-term persistent prayer. The current stirrings of God around the world have the same common denominator-intercessory prayer. How many times does that fact have to be repeated before it is acted on uniformly? Based both on God's word and the history of the church, I can guarantee you a future full of blessing and power if a proper, on-going investment is made in prayer.

The church I was raised in had a motto that said, "Invest For Eternity." That is precisely what prayer does. It seeds both the present and, even more, the future. The rewards of prayer are both here and now and then and there. There is a reaping in this life as well as the one to come.

Another point we must remember, however, is that reaping can be negative as well as positive. We've all heard the expression, "Live by the sword, die by the sword." This means that those who maim, kill, and do violence can expect to have the same things done to them. It is the fruit of that binding law of sowing and reaping. Violent acts start a cycle of lawlessness that will end in lawless deeds.

How can we obtain a positive harvest? How can we "seed" the future in prayer and intercession? How can we ensure that certain consequences embodying the will of God will happen?

First, any prayer that hopes to get an answer from God must be prayed according to his will. Prayers apart from the will of God have no hope of a response. They are equivalent to the seed in Matthew's parable that fell beside the road and birds ate them. The sowing was done, but the attempt was futile. The conditions of good sowing were not met.

How does a person determine God's will in a matter? Ask! That single word is the powerful, liberating answer to the need for wisdom. In addition, read the Word. Allow the Holy Spirit to guide your thoughts and mind and give you understanding. His witness, coupled with the Scriptures, will indicate to you what God wants.

Once you know what God wants to do, prayer becomes a partnership between God and man to release Kingdom power on earth. If we pray in believing faith, we can affect the future. We are encouraged with such verses as, "Call upon me, and I will answer" (Jeremiah 33:3

KJV); "Those that seek me... shall find me" (Proverbs 8:17 KJV); "Drawn nigh to God, and he will draw nigh to you" (James 4:8 KJV); "If any man doeth his will, him he heareth" (John 9:31 KJV).

We are often called upon to pray and then pray again. Some say repetitive prayer demonstrates little faith. The opposite is true. Repetitive praying is the same as putting a certain amount of money in the bank from every paycheck. Both money and prayer have an accrual nature. With prayer, the future gains are more secure than money saved because prayer goes to God in whom nothing is lost. The more Spirit-led and Spirit-filled prayer that is made, the more powerful and potent the investment at God's throne. What is the size of your prayer investment? How regularly do you invest? The Bible does say keep on asking.

After a season of sowing and moisturizing our prayer seeds with tears, we must leave the answer and time issues with God. They are his alone. It is good for our faith and our mind to occasionally revisit the things we have committed to him. Prayer seeds must not only be sown and watered; they must occasionally be cultivated by going over the ground of our request again. This is not a lack of faith; rather it is a demonstration of cultivating faith. A prayer journal can be useful to keep track of things prayed, answers received, and needs outstanding.

Revisiting a request refreshes our faith, refocuses our minds, replenishes our spirit, re-empowers our will, and rechecks our motives. All those are things of value. Remembrance of prayer keeps requests and needs at the forefront of our minds. If we pray according to the qualifications above, all that remains to be completed is

God's answer.

All things being equal, we do not doubt that vegetables will grow in a garden in summer or that orchards will produce fruit. We do not fret or feel anxious about the end result because natural law guarantees it. No command from the world's most powerful person can coerce an apple tree to produce apples. Sunshine, warmth, and moisture working in a healthy tree will produce apples because of natural law.

It is precisely the same in the spiritual realm. God has promised that he will answer, and it is impossible for him to lie (see Hebrews 6:18). Allow that truth to germinate in your spirit. He will answer *after* we have prayed because he is a covenant keeping God. It may be minutes, days or years but he will answer. The timing of his answer is determined by eternal purposes. Our need levels, whether real or perceived, that cause us to pressure God will not produce an answer. Nor will he hurry up at our bidding. *He chooses the when.*

Elijah's prayer to reverse the drought was repeated seven times, and yielded a palm-sized cloud. That cloud was dimensionally challenged if stacked against the great need for rain and the energy of the prophet's prayer. Big praying should produce a big answer. Or so we think. But there is a very important lesson to learn from Elijah's experience. Let us never limit our view of God's responses with a sense of depreciation. There had never been a cloud like Elijah's. There was enough water in it to reverse a three-and-a-half year drought over an entire nation. If we lived in the same circumstances I believe I would have been happy indeed with God's answer. *God's response was not limited to what Elijah and his servant saw.* The little palm-sized cloud was a sufficient resource because of God's ability to pour life through it.

A lack of answers to prayer can be traced to a lack of sowing. I would like to suggest to all who read this book that your church or fellowship organizes a prayer investment team as soon as possible. Bank in the heavenly realms; intercessory prayer seeds towards the future. What you sow, you will reap. Sow well, my dear reader, sow well!

Chapter Fifteen
How to Get Your Prayers Answered

"He hears the prayers of the righteous."
– Proverbs 15:29 (LB)

Unanswered prayer is the chief complaint when the topic of prayer is openly discussed. Frustration, disappointment, and even rage have been manifested in my presence by people who felt betrayed by God at their point of need. Praying amiss, praying at the wrong time (if that's possible), and praying out of the will of God are valid reasons for him to withhold response. He always has eternity in mind and his purposes cannot be compromised to meet what we might call an emergency in our lives.

Hebrews 5:7 offers some major insights into the prayer life of Jesus. Specifically, it speaks of his prayer life during his earthly ministry. "In the days of his flesh, he offered up both prayers and supplications with loud crying and tears to the One who was able to save him from death, and he was heard because of his piety."

"He was heard." Let that phrase settle into your

heart, spirit, and mind. What a wonderful affirmation and encouragement to prayer! Those words are filled with hope and expectation. To be heard and answered is the goal of everyone who prays.

When it comes to getting prayers answered, I believe I am like most other believers. From a multitude of prayers have come only a smattering of answers. At times I sense that my prayers are like a rocket launch–full of fire and power and rapidly on their way into the heavens. Almost from the first words uttered, I feel God's presence, praying is easy, and there seems to be little resistance from the devil. The assurance of an answer seems guaranteed. Far more frequently, however, are the times when I feel my prayers do not get beyond the ceiling of the place where I'm praying. Have you ever had that impression that your prayers did not get any further than the tip of your tongue? Have you ever said prayers that–at least to the senses–drew no presence, experienced no warfare, and appeared to gain no ground? I must confess that I have had ample experience with prayers that felt flat and fruitless.

Jesus' experience was very different. In the hope-filled words, "He was heard," we can look for the principles that he practiced and apply them to our lives. Why was he heard? How did he pray to get a response? What method did he use in bringing his earthly concerns before the Father?

Hebrews 5:7 begins with the words "in the days of his flesh," referring to the time Jesus spent in earthly ministry. *He found it necessary to pray.* As we read through the Gospels, we see the need for prayer, along with his example of prayer. Luke 5:16 describes another aspect of the prayer life of Jesus. "But he himself would often slip away into the wilderness and pray." Let those words slip deep into your spirit, especially *often, away,* and *wilderness.* Jesus was well acquainted with loneliness and isolation. His life pattern called him there often. If Jesus made going away to be alone in prayer a lifestyle, can any less be expected of us? Does your prayer pattern follow his example?

Another characteristic of the prayer life of Jesus was loud crying and tears. John 11:1-47 relates the story of the resurrection of Lazarus from his tomb in Bethany. Lazarus and his sisters were counted among the inner circle of the friends of Jesus and he was often in their home. The heart of the story is that Lazarus became ill and died. When informed of his death, Jesus did not go immediately to the family. Rather, he allowed a total of four days to pass before he went to Bethany.

Both anger and a tinge of frustration were directed towards Jesus by Martha when he finally arrived. "Lord if you had been here, my brother would not have died," she told him (John 11:21 NIV). Her response came from human affection, not spiritual discernment. After some teaching about the resurrection, the family and friends moved to the burial place, a scene of deep grieving and sorrow. When Jesus saw this, the Bible says, "He was deeply moved in spirit and troubled" (John 11:33).

Before the tomb of Lazarus, Jesus cried. He wept because he knew the unseen enemy called death was yet to be conquered. He wept because his friend had died. He wept at the hopeless attitude of his friends. I believe he also wept in some measure for the joy to come.

In John 11 :40-42 (KJV), Jesus held a conversation with his Father. Interestingly, he did not ask for power to resurrect Lazarus. Instead, he praised his Father for hearing him. Then he added, "Thou hearest me always." There it is again. Jesus was heard in heaven. Why? Because of his loud crying and tears. Ultimately, everyone who prays has one goal, to be heard by God!

Webster's dictionary defines crying as "an inarticulate utterance of distress, pain or rage." Weeping and crying give expression to the innermost and deepest feelings of the soul at a level where words are inadequate to convey the full weight of meaning. Pain and distress become compressed into the subconscious and the spirit of weeping gives expression. Crying provides ventilation.

Recall the experience of Hannah as she was being observed by Eli the priest: "Now it came about, as she continued praying before the Lord, that Eli was watching her mouth. As for Hannah, she was speaking in her heart, only her lips were moving, but her voice was not heard. So Eli thought she was drunk" (1 Samuel 1:12-13).

How little discernment Eli had when he accused a weeping woman of drunkenness when she was actually in the gripping pangs of intercession. In 1 Samuel 1:15-16 Hannah described her condition as being "oppressed of spirit." In her heaviness, she poured out her heart before the Lord. In verse 10 of this chapter she "wept bitterly." When the soul is inarticulate, weeping gives expression.

The soul of a person, the so-called inner man, is the storage area for all the emotional activities of life. It has massive capacity to experience good, bad, happy and sad emotions. Day after day and year after year, pain and joy, hurt and hilarity are gathered in the souls and retained by the memory. Everything sensory is converted into electrochemical charges that are blasted into the soft tissues of the brain. There they wait for expression and release.

He Could Have But He Didn't

Praying often centers in cries for deliverance from some distress or fulfillment of some need. Prayers are uttered in search of physical healing, freedom from oppression, deliverance from difficult circumstances, for guidance, and help of various kinds. For me, the greatest single challenge in prayer comes from those days and hours when God seems to be silent, absent, or otherwise occupied, removed and distant from my needs. My mind says he is not there. My soul languishes in loneliness. My emotions say more prayer is not worth the effort; they instruct me to stop trying to make God do something. Have you been near these circumstances at all?

What can we do in those moments? Should we believe our emotions and our intellect only? No, we must stand on God's word no matter what we think or feel.

In honor of his passion, Jesus prayed to the "one who was able" (Hebrews 5:7). That is the secret. *Prayer is made to a person,* and not to a belief system, philosophy, or ideology. Moses had to grip the revelation of the "I Am," the self-existing God. Daniel discovered his deliverance in the den, Israel in its temple, Gideon in the fleece, Paul on the Damascus road, and John on Patmos. To whom shall we flee when we are in need? "To the One who is able." To fully understand the power of prayer, every believer must somewhere and sometime have an encounter with the able One. That encounter must be wrapped in the demonstration and power of the Holy Spirit.

Jesus' life was at stake when he prayed, "My Father, if it is possible, let this cup pass from Me" (Matthew 26:30). But neither his prayer nor his relationship to the Father saved him from death. The Father could have granted the request but did not, even though at his command was all the power of the universe.

Since we know the Father is sovereign and can do as he pleases, why did he choose not to rescue his Son from the horrible death that was certainly ahead? For the same reason he does not answer the first moment we make most of our distress calls; the same reason Jesus did not immediately answer Mary and Martha's request to come quickly lest their brother die. The answer is that the Father always answers prayers in the light of eternity, and not to accommodate our comfort level.

Rescuing Jesus from his Jewish persecutors would have been a humane and noble thing to do. It would have displayed the Father's power. But the loss to mankind would have been catastrophic. If Jesus had not died, there would have been no blood sacrifice or remedy for sin. Mankind would not have a Savior. The greater good –in the light of eternity–was provided by Jesus' suffering and shame and bearing the humiliation of death on the cross. His resurrection confirmed the *rightness* of the Father's decision. His death, not his preservation, brought eternal life to mankind.

We know from Scripture and from experience that

God is able to intervene at any stage in the affairs of men. Because issues and prayer remain unanswered in many lives, we should think about approaching God differently. Instead of pestering him for the reason he has not answered, it might be wiser to discover what his will is and ask for wisdom to understand what he is telling us. Better yet, ask him what will serve the greater good; that is, what will bring him the most glory and, at the same time, be most beneficial in promoting eternal values. He can perfect our knowledge, setting forth the answers and explaining his actions. Remember the cemetery scene at Bethany? Jesus was able to reverse the curse of death, resurrect Lazarus, and use the event to teach the doctrine of the resurrection.

Hebrews 5:7 also says, Jesus was heard, "because of his piety." Some translations says "because he feared God." That phrase is the key to understanding the entire verse and to answer the question, why Jesus' prayers were answered. The term "piety" in the original Bible language is *eulabeia,* which means caution or dread. Taken to its roots, the term is from a combination of words that mean "good" and "to take hold of." It is used in the verb form and should be translated "moved with fear." To clarify understanding, the term embodies the idea of reverence for God, to take hold of God carefully and circumspectly, to move in the reverential awe of God.

What does this mean for those of us who love and pray now? *The prayers of Jesus were answered because of the quality of his character.* He lived a holy life. He regarded his Father in every deed, thought, and act, and lived his life under the fear of the Father. In the western church today, sin is lightly regarded. There is little fear of

God. And when there is no fear of God, no respect for his word, no regard for the consequences of sinful acts, no remorse for past sins, then there is little aspiration towards holiness. Thus, it is no wonder that our prayers are not answered. To be "heard" we must become more Christ-like in our fear, awe, and reverence of God.

Regardless of delays and deferrals, take solace in the fact that God is able! Even though loud crying and tears may be your condition at the moment, he is still able to make a difference in your life. As an exercise, and before you pray again, take a few minutes and enter into a worship mode before the living God who is able to deliver. He has promised that "if any man be a worshipper of God, and doeth his will, him he heareth" (John 9:31 KJV).

Chapter Sixteen
The God Who Hears and Responds

There is an awkward and silly social exchange that happens fairly regularly in our culture. It's probably happened to you many times. In fact, you've probably been on both sides of the dialogue.

Person A is visiting Person B's home. The conversation is moving along, and then the host or hostess asks the guests, "Would anyone like coffee?"

At this point there's an awkward pause, because the guest would indeed like a cup of coffee. But they feel uncomfortable asking for it, afraid that it's an imposition. So they hesitate, because the hostess raised the question. The hostess smiles, waiting for an answer. The guest wonders if this is some sort of test of their manners. After a pregnant pause, the guest responds tentatively, "Well, only if you were *already* going to make some."

The guest has actually answered the question with a question. What they are really saying to the hostess is, "Do *you* want any coffee? Do you want to make coffee? Are you going to make coffee for yourself? Because I'm only going to ask for it if you were going to give it to me anyway."

The guest feels humble and gracious, and figures the host must be impressed with their humility and politeness. Besides, since they said that their desire for coffee depends on the host's desire, the guest can't be disappointed: if they get it, great; if not, they didn't really want it anyway.

The hostess is usually irritated by this tiresome ritual. Most of the time she offered it as a gift. She would be happy to make coffee if the guest would only answer the question honestly. She rolls her eyes at the false humility.

Traveling in foreign countries on missionary trips, I have seen Americans do this with churches that were hosting them. In many cultures the hosts are perplexed, wondering, "What's wrong with these people?" I've seen hosts offended by this rejection of their hospitality, or the implication that their hospitality was a false gesture. They wanted to give a gift, to serve their guests, and felt like that was tossed back in their face.

The only thing sillier than this routine is that many people follow the same pattern in their prayer life. God asks them what they want. In a sort of misguided attempt at humility, and a desire to avoid being disappointed, they make their requests contingent on whether God was already planning on doing or giving them what they would like to ask for. *"If it's your will..."* is a strange way to start telling God what *you* want. Of course God isn't going to give you anything that contradicts his will or justice. But he didn't ask you what *he* wanted, he asked what *you* wanted. What's on *your* heart? What do you desire, or think that you need? It goes without saying that God will decide whether or not to give it to you based on his wisdom. But too many of us pretend to be humble, when we are really just protecting ourselves from getting hurt.

How we ask for something depends on what we believe about the person we are asking. If we think they are inferior to us, or owe us something, we might be demanding. If we are speaking to someone we don't know well, but would like to impress, we might be formal and especially courteous. If we are asking a big favor of someone to whom we are in debt, we might be solicitous.

What does it reveal about who we think God is when we tell him that we only want something if he was going to do it anyway? Does it prove that we have a humble, polite, respectful, and deferential character? Or does it demonstrate what we believe about his character?

In a slightly different context, Jesus tells a story about a man who misunderstood his master's character. In the Parable of the Talents, the third servant presents the one talent that his master entrusted to him safe and sound. He tells the master, "I knew that you are a hard man, harvesting where you have not sown and gathering where you have not scattered seed. So I was afraid and went out and hid your talent in the ground. See, here is what belongs to you" (Matthew 25:24-25). He expects to be congratulated for not losing it. Of course the master is angry that he didn't earn any interest on his investment, but he's furious over the insult: his servant just called him a hard-hearted, cruel thief.

Inserting, *"If it be your will..."* before a prayer request is hardly that sort of an insult, but it is a misunderstanding of God's character and the nature of the relationship he wants with us. He doesn't want us to be afraid of him. He's unlikely to say to us, *"So, you want coffee, huh? Well, I only make coffee if I feel like having some myself, and I don't feel like it right now. Frankly, I'm offended that you'd ask."* Is that the kind of God we have?

Of course not. In fact, Jesus says, "Which of you, if his son asks for bread, will give him a stone? Or if he asks for a fish, will give him a snake? If you, then, though you are evil, know how to give good gifts to your children, how much more will your Father in heaven give good gifts to those who ask him!" (Matthew 7:9-10). God is our father, who loves us very much. Perhaps some of us had earthly fathers who were not generous or kind, and we were afraid to ask them for anything. If so, we are projecting that experience on our Heavenly Father and approaching him with fear and false humility, carefully framing our requests so that we won't get disappointed.

It's sad that some of us misunderstand God that way. We shouldn't be anxious or tentative in asking him for what we want or need. Paul tells us in Philippians 4:6-7, "Do not be anxious about anything, but in everything, by prayer and petition, with thanksgiving, present your requests to God. And the peace of God, which transcends all understanding, will guard your hearts and your minds in Christ Jesus." So, if you want the coffee, just tell God!

Some of you might be saying, "Doesn't James tell us to frame our requests this way?" Actually, James doesn't say that. James 4:15 tells us that, "You ought to say, 'If it is the Lord's will, we will live and do this or that.'" But the context is not *what* we ask God for, but of how we present our plans to others. James warns us not to think that we are ultimately in control of our lives. We should be wise enough to recognize that everything is contingent on God's will, and not be so overconfident in our own schemes that we boast and brag about them.

To be fair, in the Garden of Gethsemene Jesus asks God to "let this cup pass" if it is "possible," or "in your will." But if we read the passages carefully, we see that Jesus is actually acknowledging his willingness to accept God's plan, not making his request contingent on God's will. In Matthew's version Jesus prays, "My Father, if it is possible, may this cup be taken from me. Yet not as I will, but as you will." Mark records it as, "Abba, Father... everything is possible for you. Take this cup from me. Yet not what I will, but what you will." In Luke, Jesus says, "Father, if you are willing, take this cup from me; yet not my will, but yours be done." Jesus is clear that he wishes there were some other way to accomplish God's plan, but he acknowledges that there is not, and he expresses his willingness to go along with it.

Of course we know that God may not give us what we ask for. God knows our wants and needs better than we do. He knows what we think we want, and what we really want. And he knows what we think we need, and what we really need. In his wisdom and power, he always does what is best. That should never stop us from expressing our feelings, pouring out our hearts, and asking him for want we want. But we must be mature enough to recognize that sometimes he will say, "No." Sometimes he will say, "Not yet," or "Not here," or "Not in that way."

The Lord gave Paul some sort of affliction. We don't know what it was, but he called it the "thorn in my flesh."

In 2 Corinthians 12:8-9 he says, "Three times I pleaded with the Lord to take it away from me. But he said to me, 'My grace is sufficient for you, for my power is made perfect in weakness.' Therefore I will boast all the more gladly about my weaknesses, so that Christ's power may rest on me." Paul wasn't afraid to ask for what he wanted, but he was willing to accept God turning him down.

Does God ever change his mind in response to our prayers? We sometimes hedge our prayers by saying, *"If it be your will..."* because we are afraid that God's mind is already made up, and that nothing we say can change it. But is that true? Does God ever shape his will based on what we ask for, or are we always supposed to shape our prayers around his predetermined plans?

There's at least one dramatic story in the Bible that suggests that God does consider our prayers before he acts. In Exodus 32 Moses has been up on Mount Sinai, receiving the Ten Commandments. The Israelites, camped at the base of the mountain, get tired of waiting for Moses. They build a golden calf, a pagan statue that reminded them of Egypt, and begin a noisy worship festival. God hears the commotion, and tells Moses what it is. He tells Moses, "I have seen these people...and they are a stiff-necked people. Now leave me alone so that my anger may burn against them and that I may destroy them. Then I will make you into a great nation." (Exodus 32:9-10). Moses is horrified, and pleads with God to change his mind, offering several reasons why destroying them is a bad idea. Amazingly, in verse 14, it says, "Then the LORD relented and did not bring on his people the disaster he had threatened." God changes his mind and his plans because of Moses' prayer. God considers the prayers of his people. God wants us to to ask him for what we want. Sometimes he agrees, and sometimes he doesn't. Sometimes he adjusts his plans based on his people's prayers.

Hebrews tells us that we should be even more bold than Moses was. In a direct reference to Moses and the Hebrews at Sinai, Hebrews 12:18-24 tells us that we, "have not come to a mountain that can be touched and that is burning with fire; to darkness, gloom and storm; to a trumpet blast or to such a voice speaking words that those who heard it begged that no further word be spoken to them, because they could not bear what was commanded: 'If even an animal touches the mountain, it must be stoned.' But you have come to Mount Zion, to the heavenly Jerusalem, the city of the living God. You have come to thousands upon thousands of angels in joyful assembly... to Jesus the mediator of a new covenant." The death and resurrection of Christ means that we don't need to grovel in fear before God, afraid to pray for what we want. We approach him as adopted sons, co-heirs of his glory (Romans 8:17).

We can approach God as a loving and wise Father, not a stern and stingy tyrant. He understands what it is like to live in this world, and to have wants and needs. Hebrews 4:15-16 assures us that, "We do not have a high priest who is unable to sympathize with our weaknesses, but we have one who has been tempted in every way, just as we are—yet was without sin. Let us then approach the throne of grace with confidence, so that we may receive mercy and find grace to help us in our time of need."

This is an important difference between Christ and

the concept of Allah in Islam. The word *insha'allah* is prominent in that religion. It means "If it is God's will," and Muslims say it often. The idea permeates Islam, and its notion of prayer. The Koran instructs Muslims to pray five times a day, facing the city of Mecca. The daily prayers are a formal ritual, involving ceremonial washing, the removal of shoes, the use of prayer mats, bowing, and reciting. These prayer are not intimate moments with a kind and wise Father or a risen Savior. One does not approach the throne of Allah with the kind of confidence we just read about in Hebrews 4. Muslims do not pray five times a day to ask for things, they pray to acknowledge Allah's greatness and conform themselves to his will. To use the metaphor from the beginning of this chapter, they only ask for coffee if Allah was already going to make some anyway.

We have a God who not only asks us what we want, but who also hears and responds. He won't accept our timidity, tentativeness, or false humility. He refuses to let us hang back in prayer, not asking so that we won't risk being told no. He promises that if you will engage with an open heart, he will do the same. Where might that take you? You'll have to tell him what you want to find out.

Chapter Seventeen

The Great Rewards of Hanging Tough

"Always keep on praying."
– 1 Thessalonians 5:17 (LB)

"You can never please God without faith, without depending on Him. Anyone who wants to come to God must believe that there is a God and He rewards those who sincerely look for Him."
– Hebrews 11:6 (LB)

I love stories from Africa, the so-called "dark continent." An American missionary had spent many years there and had evangelized and built churches in four nations. Yet his heart was yearning to do more. The desire to do more caused the missionary to engage in a special time of fasting and prayer. His goal was to get an answer to these questions: "What do you want me to do next? How can your work in the area where I labor increase exponentially? What changes do I need to make to become more effective?"

After some days of fasting prayer, he had some

impressions that he felt were answers to his questions. One was clear and also outside the range of his questions. God was saying something to him that he had not asked. The missionary saw a mental picture of a simple road sign that would be at the entry to any town. The sign was of the common type that sets on two legs, stands about five feet above the ground and measured three feet across and one foot high. On that sign was the name *Msangali* (pronounced "mmsangauli"). He understood Msangali to be a place, but in his thirty years of travel around Africa he could not recall ever having heard of such a place. It was certainly not listed on the best available maps.

As he continued to travel from place to place he would ask people if they knew about a place called Msangali. "Could it be a mountain or remote river somewhere? Could it be a village hidden in the rain forest?" Most people to whom his inquiries were made responded with a shrug of the shoulders. No one knew. No one had heard of Msangali.

After three years, the discovery of Msangali came in a very easy way. An American pastor came to visit his missionary friend, to dedicate a Bible school and preach at a few crusades. While having lunch in a small town, the missionary posed his question to the waiter, "Have you ever heard of Msangali?" "Yes", he said. "I know that place. A few years ago I lived nearby but as soon as I could, I moved away. It is a terrible place." "Why is it not on the best maps?" the missionary asked. The waiter responded with a long answer. "The place is full of criminals, robbers, prostitutes and evil men of every sort. Every day people are stabbed and killed. Many criminals go there after serving their prison sentences because their own towns and villages reject them. While in prison they hear that Msangali is a lawless place with almost no police presence. The governor of the area serves only because he has agreed not to interfere unduly with the criminal activity." The missionary wanted to know if there were any churches there. "No," said the waiter, "No one has preached in Msangali for more than twenty-five years. It is too dangerous. And the people will reject them anyway. It is a dark place."

Msangali sounded like the kind of challenge the missionary had prayed and hoped for. Two days later he took the American pastor to see the governor. They found Msangali to be a coastal town of about 30,000 inhabitants. There was only one road leading in and out through a small mountain pass, and it was geographically isolated from its neighbors. The missionary asked the governor for permission to hold a gospel crusade there. After many verbal warnings and with much hesitancy, the governor granted his request.

Some weeks later a large tent was erected in a central location in the town. An African evangelist and his team arrived to hold a crusade since the American pastor had to return to his home. The results were immediate and outstanding. Hundreds accepted Christ and many were healed from many types of maladies. The crusade lasted for two months, and during that time a group of seven ladies came to the missionary and identified themselves as intercessors who had prayed faithfully for Msangali. They had met weekly in a house for more than twenty years to pray for their town. They had sent inquiries and invitations to many evangelists and missionary groups seeking help, but none had responded, or they were too afraid to come. But the praying seven held to the idea that those who pray will, one day, get an answer. So they remained resolute and determined. After twenty years, God answered.

The Prayers of Hannah

This story is of another lady who prayed persistently. May her example of prayer become yours and mine. Her name is Hannah. Like the ladies above she prayed years before God answered. Furthermore, she was seriously hassled by her husband's other wife and by the culture of her day which branded an infertile woman as being disfavored by God. But Hannah persisted and her triumph was wonderfully rewarded beyond her expectations.

If you have prayed a long time about a matter and have not, as yet, received an answer, you will understand intimately Hannah's pain, frustration and agony. Her story is a revelation regarding the process of long-term, repetitive praying. Coupled with perseverance, that process brought one of the most amazing answers to prayer in the entire Bible, though it was costly and time consuming.

An axiom that affects everyone who prays states: *The longer we pray about a matter without an answer, the stronger the tendency is for our faith to decline.* Conversely, penetrating prayer will actually fuel our faith, keep Jesus at the center of our search, and energize our hope. Hannah is one of the most significant models of this kind of praying.

Her Name

The three main characters in 1 Samuel 1 and 2 are Elkhanah (meaning God has obtained or possessed) and his two wives Penninah (round like a pearl or coral colored) and Hannah. Hannah's name means "God has obtained or favored." But there is more. Another word related to her name that helps us understand her as a person and intercessor is *canah,* which means "to stoop or bend in kindness to an inferior." This character strength is seen in Hannah's lack of retaliation towards Penninah who "would provoke her bitterly to irritate her" (1 Samuel 1:6). Another related term from the core of her name, *chnanah,* means "to pitch a tent, for abode or siege or prayer or war." In English we might say it this way, "I have come with a goal and purpose in my heart, have put down a stake, and will not leave until I get what I came for."

Taken together, these words describe a God-possessed woman, full of destiny and purpose whose character was marked by humility, resilience, and perseverance. The Bible says of Hannah, "Year after year she went up to the house of the Lord." She pitched her tent at God's door and determinedly revisited her request till it was answered.

As a child I remember hearing older saints speak of a "made up mind." I believe they were defining the prayer character of Hannah. *Focused* and *determined* are other words that describe her prayer mode. Though God did not show himself to her quickly, she intuitively knew the principle Jeremiah wrote about: "Call to me, and I will answer you" (Jeremiah 33:3). Her personal needs and her knowledge of God's benevolent character challenged Hannah to pray. Her right heart, teamed with faith and persistence, caused her to know without reservation that God would respond.

Suffering, Praying, and No Answer

Praying long term without a timely answer is genuinely distressing and can be eroding to our faith. The perception of our need becomes more intense when days turn into years of waiting for an answer. "Year after year" Hannah waited for an answer to her prayers (1 Samuel 1:7). To make the situation worse, Elkanah's second wife had children, and made it her occupation to criticize and despise Hannah because of her barren condition. Every year it was the same. Penninah scoffed, mocked, and belittled, while Hannah wept. 1 Samuel 1:7 says, "And it happened year after year, as often as she went up to the house of the Lord, she would provoke her, so she wept and would not eat."

The word used in the original text for Penninah's provoking action was *ka'ac* which means "to trouble." In plain language, Hannah hurt so badly her appetite was gone.

Prayer is often like war. Life becomes even more difficult when, in addition to the spiritual resistance in the heavenly realms, you are being treated unjustly by those close to you. It is also harder to face when the trouble you are experiencing is not the consequence of sin. Remember, the Lord had "closed her womb." Do you think the accuser may have taken advantage of the situation?

I have been privileged to travel and meet believers all over the world in my journeys. I have discovered that a great many believers around the world have suffered and some are suffering now under illegitimate governmental powers, ruled by tyrants and despots or "isms" such as Communism. These people suffer for no reason other than they are preaching the gospel and loving Jesus. David spoke about this in Psalm 57:4:

> *"My soul is among lions;*
>
> *I must lie among those who breathe forth fire,*
>
> *Even the sons of men, whose teeth are spears and arrows,*
>
> *and their tongue a sharp sword."*

Have you ever felt that way? Through the years, I have spoken to many men who have experienced long prison sentences for Jesus' sake. One man was arrested in the middle of the night for witnessing to a friend about his deliverance from alcoholism. He was ripped away from three young sons under the age of seven and taken to prison in Siberia. Unbeknownst to this believer or his wife was the fact she was three months pregnant with their fourth child when he was taken away. The man spent eleven years in solitary confinement. When he was released in 1990, he learned that his wife had died in childbirth and he met a son he had not known existed. Unjust? Yes. A thousand times yes! Wrong? In every way! Was he bitter? Amazingly no. He was thrilled that the time had finally come when he could freely preach the gospel. Lesser men become bitter. Real saints become better. Hannah's long term praying affected her in positive ways. Her faith increased, her spirit and heart were tender before the Lord, and her patience level increased exponentially because of persistent prayer made during a season of personal persecution.

"Why are you in despair, O my soul?

And why have you become disturbed within me?

Hope in God, for I shall yet praise him

The help of my countenance, and my God."

– (Psalm 42:11)

"Why then be downcast? Why be discouraged and sad?

Hope in God! I shall yet praise him again. Yes, I shall again

Praise him for his help."

– (Psalm 42:4-5)

Agony of Divine Silence

Hannah's destiny is best described in these words: "Penninah had children, but Hannah had no children" (1 Samuel 1:2). Again, "The Lord had closed her womb" (1 Samuel 1:5-6). *The "womb closing" is a signal that indicates God was up to something so big, he was willing to controvert natural law to bring it to pass.*

In the time of Hannah, childlessness was considered a form of God's judgment, and it brought civil, religious and societal disfavor. The culture and religion of the day were inextricably mixed, and it all worked against Hannah as well. Add to that the sense that God was distant and not listening and you can understand the weight of distress parked on Hannah's life. Her biological clock was ticking, but God did not seem to care.

Hannah did what all good Jews did. At least once a year she visited the Temple. She was aware of God's mighty works, yet heard no audible voice, and she prayed but saw no tangible response. Jesus also felt the agony of divine silence. He found it at the cross. What feelings are expressed by these words, "Why have you forsaken me?" Habakkuk sensed the same when he asked, "How long, Oh Lord, will I call for help and thou wilt not hear?" (Habakkuk 1:2). David also felt that same sense of abandonment. Listen to his words:

> *"My wounds grow foul and fester.*
>
> *Because of my folly,*
>
> *I am bent over and greatly bowed down;*
>
> *I go mourning all day long.*
>
> *For my loins are filled with burning;*
>
> *And there is no soundness in my flesh.*
>
> *I am benumbed and badly crushed;*
>
> *I groan because of the agitation of my heart."* – (Psalm 38:5-8).

Or again in Psalms 22:1:

> *"My God, my God why hast Thou forsaken me?*
>
> *Far from my deliverance are the words of my groaning."*

The Process of Prayer Distillation

From Hannah, we learn some of the most keen insights into repetitive, long-term praying in the entire Bible.

"And she, being greatly distressed, prayed to the Lord and wept bitterly."

– (1 Samuel 1:10)

What exactly is "bitter praying" and what can be learned from Hannah's experience? The word *bitter* has its roots in the term *marab,* the place of bitterness. The root of *marab* is *mar* which means to drip or distill. It is a term developed in ancient Arabia to describe the production of alcohol or the distillation of spirits.

In its simplest form, boiling grain, yeast, and sugar produces a form of alcohol. The vapor ascends into a curled pipe called a cooling coil. There the vapor cools, reconstitutes to a liquid, and is collected in a second container. The recovered liquid is largely alcohol. Via chemical processes, when heated the grain and other ingredients change into alcohol.

The distilling process, taking the recovered liquid and boiling it, is repeated. That which is collected from each repeated heating, cooling and recovery becomes purer and more powerful. Those are the key words, *purer and more powerful.* Every reprocessing improves the quality of the alcohol.

The term "distill" is used to describe Hannah's praying. The repeated nature of her prayers caused her motives to be purer and her praying more powerful as she prayed year after year. Think of the possibilities! Spirit-anointed, God-centered praying becomes more powerful in its repetition. Any motive other than God's glory was purged from Hannah in this years-long process.

At first Hannah simply prayed for a child. Later she became more focused and asked for a man-child. After years of asking, she promised God that any child he would give to her she would give back to him for temple service and ministry. It was then that God responded and Samuel was conceived.

The Needs of God

Why was Samuel conceived after being promised to God for ministry? God has needs that are met through, and only through, his people. Because of those needs, and because he always has eternity in mind, he responds to prayer in terms of how his answers further implement the growth and development of his eternal kingdom.

Lou Engle says, "The task of prayer is to get our hearts aligned with his."[5] We have seen clearly God preventing the birth of a child through Hannah. That should be a clue that something grand is in the making, and he is behind it all. Something great will be coming for both Hannah and God in which both have a major stake and gain.

During Hannah's life, the spiritual leadership over Israel was in steep decline. The high priest Eli and his sons had become lax in integrity, morality, worship, and pastoral care for the people. The house of Eli was in rapid decline. In the midst of the decline, God heard a praying woman asking for a child which he knew she would, after many years, finally surrender to him for service in the temple. When Hannah's purified prayer met God's need in the heavenlies, she conceived. A few months later she had her son and God had a new leader in the making.

One of the great keys in getting prayer answered is to be in agreement with God's eternal purposes. Something of national significance was being worked in and through Hannah. The stressful delays were of divine origin. In the process of time, Samuel was born, the first of a new type of leader. As a child he was in the temple but he was not an ordinary child doing temple tasks. He was the first man to carry a triple anointing for service as a prophet, judge, and priest. There had not been a man like him in all the history of Israel. Would you like to have been the parent of that child?

The lonely, agonizing hours of prayer are the process God uses to purify our motives and align our hearts with his. It takes time to distill the pure things God wants. But I ask you, was Hannah's wait worth it?

Chapter Eighteen
Be Bold, Ask Largely

"The Archimedean point outside the world is the little chamber where a true supplicant prays in all sincerity, where he lifts the world off its hinges."
– Soren Kierkegaard

"The Lord is far from the wicked, but he hears the prayers of the righteous."
– Proverbs 15:29 (LB)

The praying of Elijah the prophet

Only a few men and women are entrusted with intercession responsibilities that immediately and directly affect entire nations. Every intercessor improves the overall spiritual climate and fulfilling of the purposes of God, but certain people have specific prayer assignments over nations. Elijah was one. He also was a prophet and his ministry, which was under-girded and supported by intercession, was accompanied by miracles.

Elijah's story begins in 1 Kings 17. There we learn his family name, his name, and his birthplace. Beyond those few details, nothing is said of his history. One defining moment, however, introduces us to this Old Testament giant of faith. It is the moment in which Elijah first meets King Ahab and delivers a strong, prophetic word of forthcoming judgment in the form of drought. This predicted drought was to begin immediately and would last until the people repented. Elijah professed to King Ahab that he was the only person on earth with the authority to reverse the drought conditions. Here is the word of the Lord: "There shall not be dew nor rain these years, but according to my word" (1 Kings 17:1 KJV). If you had been King Ahab, what would you have thought? What would you have done?

The scenario of impending judgment, along with an intractable prophet and the prophet's clear awareness of his own importance had to be a difficult time for Ahab. He did, of course, deserve such difficulty. The predicted scene of judgment had been birthed in prayer and the scope and reach of it was national.

What gave Elijah the strength, self-understanding, words, and resolve to do what he did and say what he said? Seeing his identity in God via intercession, he reported, "The Lord God of Israel liveth, before whom I stand" (1 Kings 17:1 MV). By revelation and inward illumination, he knew the ground upon which he stood.

The phrase, "before whom I stand" unlocks insight into Elijah. First it implies Elijah was accepted by God. Second, it speaks of his willingness to go to God in a bold, confident way. Third, Elijah knew if he had entrance and acceptance before God, he would also have answers to his petitions. Any person who knows how to reach God and get a response is a threat to the purveyors of unrighteousness, even up to and including those who lead

Before whom I stand

nations.

While little is known of Elijah's background and history, more is known about Ahab. 1 Kings 16:30 says, "Ahab the son of Omri did evil in the sight of the Lord more than all who were before him." Following is a short list of his evil activities as found in 1 Kings 16:

- walked in the sin of Jeroboam (verse 31).
- married Jezebel (verse 31).
- served and worshipped Baal (verse 31).
- built an altar for Baal (verse 32).
- made the Ashram-wooden symbols of female deities (verse 33).

Ahab had forgotten God. But apparently he had not forgotten that Jehovah was different from all other gods. Jehovah claimed to be the "I AM," the self-existing, ever-living, supreme God, and because he is the living God, he sees, hears, and speaks. Jehovah had taken note of the altars constructed for Baal worship, the hard hearts of the people, and the wickedness of the leadership. Through Elijah, he spoke judgment to Ahab's kingdom.

God always enlists the partnership of people. Elijah was a qualified partner in furthering righteousness in Israel because of his holy heart, his passion for righteousness, his intercession, and his willingness to let God work out the answers to the things he prayed for. We know from James 5 that seven sessions or prayer attempts were needed to reverse the drought conditions. Elijah's early prayers had "shut up the heavens." Persistent, passionate, long-term praying brought in the drought judgment. The same was required to reopen the heavens.

As a direct result of spiritual intercession, God touched Israel in the realm of the natural. Drought! Effective intercession, since it has a negative and positive aspect, stops things as well as releases them. Depending on the situation, we must be willing to pray both ways, for or against, to close or open. Following the drought was pestilence (an invasion of insects that eat crops); and following the pestilence was a famine caused by the lack of food production. In the midst of the famine, Ahab had the nerve to call Elijah the "troubler of Israel." Really now! Additional insight into Elijah's praying is found in James 5:16b-18:

> *"The effective prayer of a righteous man can accomplish much. Elijah was a man with a nature like ours, and he prayed earnestly that it might not rain and it did not rain on the earth for three years and six months. And he prayed again, and the sky poured rain, and the earth produced its fruit."*

Elijah was constrained by human nature like all humans, even those called to a high profile public ministry. He asked boldly and largely and through his prayers, controlled the destiny of a nation.

The Nature of a Praying Man

John 9:31 tells us that God does not hear sinners, except of course when they repent. The person with known sin in his life will not have his prayers heard by God, unless those prayers are repenting of sins. By contrast, the godly man will have the privilege of being heard by God and his prayer will "accomplish much" because of his proper relationship with God. The righteous man partners with God in bringing Kingdom power and presence from heaven to earth. His prayers are free of self-promotion and self-interest.

Prayer is work. Efficient prayer–the type that touches God and brings his response, the type that changes people and circumstances–is hard work. Energy is expended. Prayers that dramatically affect nations may require long hours of lonely intercession before an answer is received.

Years ago in a camp meeting, I heard a faith building story of answered prayer told through the sobs of an evening speaker. The minister spoke of his impassioned praying for his daughter who had gone spiritually awry. He locked himself alone in his bedroom for twenty-five days and nights. On the twenty-fifth day his daughter was reconciled to God. That is toil-filled, laborious praying; when practiced by a godly person, much good results.

1 Kings depicts Elijah, our man of God, at his best and his worst. In 1 Kings 18, Elijah called the entire nation to repentance. Fire fell from heaven on an animal sacrifice to validate and confirm God was with him. It was one of the great revivals in history, as the entire nation repented in a single day and returned to walking in relationship with God.

When there is an action initiated by God, be assured it will be challenged from hell. In 1 Kings 19, Queen Jezebel, the nemesis of Elijah, issued an order that the prophet be killed. Elijah's powerful praying and the demonstration of miraculous fire had destroyed Jezebel's

... because of his proper relationship w/ God

religious system and her control over the people. She, for one, was not pleased with revival.

Elijah's fiery altar of victory resulted in a fiery trial of persecution, so he fled, fearing for his life. In just a few days he slid from the high place of restoring a nation to God to the lowly estate of a fear-filled wanderer. He was bold as a lion on the upside, but on the downside easily depressed and emotionally paralyzed. His despair was so deep that he prayed to die, taking little notice of angelic visitations and other phenomena such as windstorms, earthquakes, and fire. His highs were very high and his lows extremely low. Have you ever been both to the mountaintop *and* to the pit within a short timeframe? Such is not a foreign experience to intercessors.

Because of God's faithful dealings with Elijah, he eventually was given a fresh ministry commission. But his fear-driven flight greatly diminished his prophetic and miracle ministry, although some of both still manifested through the remainder of his life. Under this new commission, God instructed him to do three things. These are found in I Kings 19:15-17:

- Anoint Hazael king over Syria (verse 15).

- Anoint Jehu king over Israel (verse 16).

- Anoint Elisha, son of Shophot, as prophet in your place (verse 17).

From the above list, Elijah completed only the number three task. The anointing for ministry was transferred to another. Elijah's potential destiny did not change, but his level of effectiveness and his fruitfulness did change–and in a major way. Because he did not respond correctly to Jezebel's threats or God's many attempts to speak to him, God selected someone else in his place. No one is indispensable to the work of God but everyone can show their potential by quick and thorough obedience.

Human nature is always at war with the Spirit. That's another reason prayer is often difficult and opposed by demonic forces. Through the study of God's Word, the power of the Holy Spirit, and the fellowship of the saints, we can ask God daily to deal with our humanness. Otherwise, after enjoying the euphoria of a Mt. Carmel-like experience, we may retreat quickly to spiritual deserts, never to return fully intact to fulfill the destiny to which we have been called and assigned. Immediately after a great triumph, we must take great care with our spirit person. Even in lonely places, Elijah's confession was, "I have done all these things at thy word" (1 Kings 18:36). Yet his fruitfulness was small when compared to his earlier ministry and God's plan for his life.

Faith-Filled Prayer and Action

1 Kings 18:20-40 records the showdown between Elijah and the priests of Baal on Mt. Carmel. It never really was a contest. However, the hoopla went on all day long with the priests of Baal doing their best to get a response from a god who never lived.

Finally it was Elijah's turn. As a first matter he repaired the altar that had been polluted and damaged during the Baal practices earlier in the day. That completed, Elijah poured several pitches of water on the sacrificial animal and asked God to show himself. Fire came from heaven, visible to everyone there. What a moment! I would loved to have been there.

Notice I Kings 18:41: "Now Elijah said to Ahab, 'Go up, eat and drink; for there is the sound of the roar of a heavy shower.'" As soon as the water soaked altar was touched by God's fiery presence, three powerful consequences followed. First, all Israel turned to the Lord. Second, the false system of religion sponsored by and used by Jezebel collapsed. Third, the drought was broken. The water on the altar was a prophetic signal of rains to come. Prophets see and hear things before they happen and when Elijah heard the "sound of a heavy shower," he announced to Ahab that rain was imminent.

From the beginning of his prayer time, Elijah had a servant present who scanned the sky for the answer to the prophet's prayers. The focused act of having someone look diligently for an answer while prayers are being prayed is a sign of a faith-filled, expectant heart. Elijah prayed with his face towards the ground, but his heart and faith were looking heavenward. The servant kept his eyes open "toward the sea," the direction from which rain normally came. *It is important where you focus when you pray.* Elijah did not have the slightest doubt God would answer, although he did not know when. This great prophet prayed repeatedly, fervently, laboriously, and earnestly. His praying seemed to be an unbroken, seamless supplication, punctuated by reports and updates from his observant servant. Again, this is faith-filled praying.

Seven times the prophet asked his servant for a report. Six times there was nothing to report. On the seventh, the servant saw something that appeared to him as insignificant, but he brought the report to Elijah anyway. "Behold, a cloud as small as a man's hand is coming up from the sea" (1 Kings 18:44). Was a little cloud all that the most influential prophet in Israel could produce with his long, heated praying?

The Cloud Principle

It is very important to understand and value the cloud principle. By any human measure, the palm-sized cloud could not contain enough water to care for a residential lawn or one thirsty person. At that point in time, the entire nation was parched. The cloud looked ridiculously inadequate in terms of both Elijah's praying and the need for moisture. But Elijah kept hearing showers and smelling rain. What followed? James 5:18 tells us, "The sky poured rain and the earth produced its fruit." *God took the insignificant and made it significant. That is the cloud principle.* Through intercession little becomes much. Big prayers sometimes produce 'little cloud' answers. But those miracle clouds are engineered in heaven to meet the need at hand.

I believe many of us have had answers to prayer that we did not recognize because what God sent seemed so miniscule in the light of the need. Perhaps God's response did not meet our expectations or was not what we anticipated. We tend, in those moments, to cast away the very thing God sent in response to our prayers. Let us not be without discernment in seeing, or unthankful in spirit or attitude for that which comes from God. Great oak trees come from tiny acorns and nations are well watered by hand sized clouds.

Mode of Prayer

After the Mt. Carmel experience, in 1 Kings 18:42 we see Elijah again humbling himself in prayer. His bodily posture was indicative of his heart attitude–bent down to the ground with his head between his knees, his eyes looking into the dirt. He was utterly dependent on God. On one occasion he prayed on Mount Carmel for fire from God and God answered. Now he was seeking God again and for something very important. It is wise to revisit those places where we have had encounters with God. Meet him again at the same place, if possible.

Intercession is a womb in which God creates life and ministry. Elijah had seen God work in enough ways to become acquainted with his character. He knew God would keep his word, reverse his judgment, and send the blessing of rain. So, in advance, and with no more than a palm-sized cloud, he announced that torrents of rain were on the way! Genuine faith speaks of things that are not yet as though they are. The nation had languished in drought and famine for three-and-a-half years. The prophets of Baal had been challenged, defeated, and killed. The people of Israel had returned to God en masse–all as a result of persistent intercession, and faith filled prayer. He asked largely. He asked boldly and he was answered.

The Consequences of Elijah's Praying

The consequences of Elijah's praying can be seen in two dimensions–natural and spiritual. His ministry joined the material with the spiritual. His prayers were mighty before God in the encounter with the prophets of Baal. As a result, Elijah converted a water soaked altar into a fiery cauldron. The resources of heaven touched earth in a tangible way; a physical altar blazed with divine fire from the non-material world.

The second consequence of Elijah's praying touched the natural and brought forth a rainstorm that replenished the entire land with moisture. Both answers to prayer were amazing physical phenomena unleashed from the spirit realm.

Reflections

I cannot help but wonder what would happen if *hundreds of believers* were to pray until God manifested himself. We could be beneficially touched in our homes, churches, and nations by both floods and fire from heaven. Recently a local church prayed for several years for an outpouring of the Holy Spirit. God came to visit and thousands of people found Christ as a result. Pray on, dear reader, pray on! Intercession makes a difference in the lives and environment of all who pray!

Chapter Nineteen
Some Who Persevered

"He who overcomes, I will make him a pillar in the temple of my God."
– Revelation 3:12

"He who overcomes, I will grant to him to sit down with Me on my throne."
– Revelation 3:21

"He who overcomes shall inherit these things, and I will be His God, and He will be God, and he will be My son."
– Revelation 21: 7

"Great works are performed not by strength, but by perseverance."
– Samuel Johnson

"By perseverance the snail reached the ark."
– Charles Spurgeon

Among church crowds there are always stories about the grandmas and grandpas who had reputations for prayer–and sometimes for their enthusiastic praise as well. Mostly one hears about the grandmas. Even though the stories are told in humorous ways, the core information comes to *this grandma knew how to pray!* Through the years I have been acquainted with a few of these prayer warriors personally and a few others through their friends or families. Inevitably, I have been the one strengthened and blessed by hearing the stories of trial and triumph, pain and pressure, challenge and conquering–all of it through prevailing, persistent prayer.

Mother Mac

A pastor told me about a lady known as "Mother Mac" with great affection and respect. She was a large woman, had a dozen kids she successfully managed with a voice barely above a whisper, and was married to a man with a drinking problem. The demands of so many children and her husband's drinking problem kept the family poor. Mother Mac was often physically abused by her intemperate husband. Church members remember seeing her with bruises on her face and arms, but she paid little attention to the bruises and went to church anyway.

During one of my ministry trips to her home church, I noticed her kneeling in a pre-service prayer meeting. She was kneeling on a folding chair near the corner of the room. It was a memorable and awesome experience. I knelt near her hoping to hear her pray. No sound could be heard, but a presence could be felt several feet away. Subjective reactions are always hard to explain with word descriptions. The most accurate description would be something akin to having your face toward a wood-burning stove roaring with a heady fire. There was a

you are called to carry the presence of Jesus

physical sense of heat that could be felt more than a yard away.

Years passed before I visited that church again. When I did go it was for a midweek service. Mother Mac's church had had its beginnings in a converted saloon. It had grown steadily into a church with more than two thousand in attendance, a large church campus, multi-pastor staff, a fully graded school, and daily radio and television broadcasts. The midweek service in that church was a "full on" meeting with large crowds and a strong sense of God's presence.

After the service a slightly built "little old lady" shuffled up to me and said something I could not hear. When I looked closer, I noticed I was looking into the ninety-two year old face of Mother Mac. She was small now and hunched over. Age and illness had taken a bodily toll. Her voice had always been like a whisper and now was nearly inaudible. But there was a message in her eyes as well as her mouth. There was fire in those penetrating eyes.

I asked her to repeat what she said and drew close to her mouth to hear. "All of this," she said, "all of this." With her right hand gesturing around at the building she repeated, "All of this, what you see here today, I saw fifty years ago in a prayer meeting and have not failed to pray everyday since." She continued her raspy comments with, "I can go home now. All that you see is what God showed me and promised me in prayer fifty years ago. It is here now, so I can go." In her mind, mission accomplished.

Where are the Mother Mac's today? Intercessors that will not stop petitioning him, paying little regard to their own needs (some of which may be huge). The burdens of life press upon them but they still seek the city set on a hill. The unique band of intercessors presses the prayer battle relentlessly. Their strength seems to grow with the length of their praying. They are not diminished by long-term intercession. They seem to find solace and energy therein.

Imagine! One woman prayed for fifty years to see something come into reality, into the physical world, that she had seen as a prayer perception. It is hard to fathom the entire good coming from this one person's prayer. *People who pray are a treasure both to God and people!*

From Latin America

I called for directions to the church. The secretary's English and my Spanish were at the same level, lacking. My request for an English speaker was soon filled by one of the church's pastors. His directions were interesting. He said the church staff was so busy leading people to Christ they had not had time to put a sign or address numbers on their building. The question was, "How do we find you?" We were instructed to locate a large hotel, stand on the front steps and from there visually locate a large beige building on an adjoining street. That would be the church. We did find the church following those directions.

When we drove past it, we noticed several couples outside on the sidewalk next to the building. We soon found ourselves inside a building with a seating capacity of several thousand. In a third world city, to have possession of such an expansive building and property was a miracle. My immediate question was, "How did all this happen?" We were soon introduced to the senior pastor who would give us the answer. He was a man in his early sixties with white hair, a gracious manner, and soft spoken. From his first words, we concluded he was passionate about prayer and evangelism.

He told us the story of how the church obtained the building. It had been constructed as a sports venue and came up for sale. The church made an acceptable offer and moved in. They had no money beyond the down payment. In terms of US dollars, the cost was in the millions. Through fasting and prayer, the twenty five percent down payment came in from people in several different countries. The congregation had one year to pay the remainder. Within one month of the settlement date, the seller's agent had the right to inspect the church finances to see if the church would be able to perform as promised.

From the seller's side of the transaction came lawyers and accountants to inspect the church's finances. To their amazement, there was almost no money in the church account. I gasped and asked the pastor why they had not been more diligent in fundraising. He simply said, "We forgot about the payment. Many people were being saved, we were also remodeling the building, purchasing equipment and re-carpeting. We just forgot about the payment."

The seller's agent had brought a back up proposal with him. In fact, the government wanted the building for a television production studio. The church could have all its money back with interest, there would be no future litigation over failing to pay the debt, and a few thousand dollars would be tossed in for good will. So the church had an "out" if it wanted or needed one. But the pastor said he believed God wanted the church to occupy the building for Jesus' sake, so he refused the offer. All monies were due in thirty days and the amount was in the millions of dollars.

How could the church pay a huge bill in thirty days with no money and very little human hope of raising it? There was not enough money in the congregation to handle the bill. There was not enough money in the entire third world city to pay the obligation. Prayer–prevailing non-stop prayer–was the answer. As they began to pray, the heavens began to open and money started pouring in from all over the world. At the due date, all the money had arrived and it came from eleven different nations. This huge provision of money is a modern day miracle and another proof of the power and influence of prevailing prayer.

There is much more to this church than the building. The place is a ministry beehive. Remember those couples on the sidewalk in front of the church? These couples, of which ninety-nine percent are non-churched, were waiting for marital counseling. The church is so successful in getting marriages repaired, that their city pays the church to counsel up to fifteen hundred people per month. The great majority of them receive Christ in the process.

There is much more. What is the power supply, the spiritual engine that energizes this church? It is the prayer room and the intercessors. Our visit was in the morning, a little before noon. We were guided to a prayer room in which dozens of men and women were praying. The pastor apologized that they prayed only twenty hours a day and not many were praying the day we visited. But there were more than two hundred people praying. "The goal," he said, "is prayer twenty-four hours a day, seven days a week."

We were also invited to view a property near town on which the church was planning a prayer center and conference facility. Both would operate twenty-four hours a day. A local businessman, a non-Christian, visited with the senior pastor and offered the church the parcel of land which his family had owned for several years. It was useless for development because of the lack of water and the family did not want to continue paying taxes on land they could not eventually develop.

The parcel was about twenty acres, not far from town. It had a high, desert-like mesa lying in the center. The church began to pray earnestly for the favor of God to come on that land. A few months later, a high grade sand and gravel deposit was located on one side of the property. On the other side of the mesa, a well was drilled and sweet water flowed in abundance. With these discoveries, the land was worth millions of dollars. The sale of sand and gravel is now providing funds for a retreat center, a meeting arena, and a prayer center to house several hundred intercessors simultaneously.

If you are in leadership in a local church, may I encourage you to personally give prayer a high profile, be an active participant and pray. Don't just tell people they should and need to. Lead by example. When God answers, celebrate the successes together that he has won.

Some questions to ask to assess your local church's prayer participation: How many minutes a month is your church prayer area occupied? What percentage of your congregation attends a prayer meeting one time per week or more? Whatever your prayer level is at the moment, what could be done to improve the situation?

Another Town and People Who Pray

I was the plenary speaker at minister's event that had been in progress all week. The venue was a very rustic camp facility. During those days one of the local pastors asked if I would come to his church on Sunday evening for ministry since his town was on the way back to the capital city, the place of my next appointment. I agreed and on Sunday afternoon my missionary host and I traveled to that town and checked into a motel and went for a swim. It was nearly seven in the evening when the missionary said, "I think we should go to church." I protested since we were in Latin America and 8:30 pm would normally be the right time to go. Things *always seemed* to start late in Latin America. The missionary took no notice of my remark and simply asked me to get ready for church as he exited the pool. I had been in that town two years prior and the local church only had 25-30 people in it, all of them quite depressed. So, I was not in a hurry to go to church. Being in that town, at least in my thinking, was just a matter of clerical courtesy.

A surprise awaited me. When we walked out of the front of our motel, I saw people coming down the side streets with Bibles in their hands. I wondered where they all could be going. Surely they were not going to the depressed church? To my shock and surprise that is exactly where they were headed. That little, ineffective, depressed church had a new building with seven hundred seats. It was already full and people were standing against the walls. Children were seated on the floor. Years before, they had one pitiful guitar player to lead worship. This night there were fifteen people playing musical instruments. The congregation was ablaze with life.

After a three-hour service, we were asked to the pastor's home for a meal. The pastor had been a businessman. When the former pastor had taken a position in another town and there was no one to look after the church, he volunteered. I wanted to know what had caused all the new life and progress. My first question was "What happened here since I saw you last?" The pastor said he just could not bear the deadness and dearth any longer in the church. But he did not know what to do. One night in the midst of emotional despair, he sensed he should arise and pray at 4:00 a.m. everyday. He also presented this challenge to his people. Only three responded.

The four of them started to pray and in a few weeks the church started to grow. New people started to come and some were not even sure why they there. Others said they had wanted to come for years and suddenly they were released to attend. One family had been dressed and prepared to attend several times and found they could not leave their home. After the praying began they were released, attended church and were converted to Christ. The church had never had so many young people. There is a college in that town and just as suddenly as they saw the things that were happening, young college students began to attend and many of them were born again.

Since the old building was inadequate and small, plans were made for a new building. Their property was large enough for a new building but they had no funds for construction. Praying produced either building supplies or the finances to buy them. No monies came from America or elsewhere. All the money needed to build came from persistent hours of intercession.

The testimony of the pastor and some of his leaders sharing the meal was simple. They said they had nowhere to turn but to God. No one offered help so they prayed. They had no money but they had faith in God and in God's word. "If you seek me I will answer" was the verse they quoted over and over. Again and again we were told "all you see is buildings and equipment and people, God sent to us. The life of this church is the product of prayers being answered."

Can that testimony be said of your church and/or ministry?

Then There are These Two

There are certain people who impact your life deeply. Here are two who touched mine. The first is Ms. Harriet. The scene of an incredible encounter with God was at a youth night with more than 700 teens present. No matter what the leaders were trying to do from the platform, there was a "buzz" all over the building. About half the teens were talking, gazing around the room, wandering in and out to the restrooms and paying little attention to the service leadership. The other half of the audience was only slightly engaged by the service.

The program that night included two musical guests and a speaker from another state. The host church in which the youth event was held was conducting special services of its own and their guest speaker was a lady less than five feet tall with white hair. She joined the other guests on the platform.

After more than an hour of noisy music, fun and games, and guest appearances, a prayer time was announced. Ms. Harriet, the little white-haired lady, was going to lead in prayer. Frankly, she seemed more than a little out of place for a teen meeting. But Ms. Harriet was there and seemed unruffled by the scene before her.

She stepped to the microphone and just said nothing. Quickly the room became quiet. With one hand grasping the microphone stand, she gazed upward with eyes wide-open but saying nothing. No words. No commands. She was just quiet before God. I watched her and my watch as well. After a full three minutes, quiet weeping could be heard in the church. After seven minutes, Ms. Harriet uttered three words. "Thank you Father." With those words, she returned to her seat and sat down.

I am sure no one was prepared for what followed. It seemed like another long minute went by and the weeping increased. No platform leaders tried to redirect the service. No musicians played. It was a moment of holy awe. There was a continual increase in weeping and praying. First one by one and then in larger groups, teens streamed to the front of the church to refresh their relationship with God. Repenting and weeping went on till midnight.

I ask you, what explains the turn in that meeting from casualness and irreverence to weeping and repentance in less than ten minutes without preaching or saying a convicting word? What gave the rise and life to those words, "Thank you, Father"? What did those words release when spoken?

Power was released and from whence did it come? The answer, of course, is long-term intercession and waiting in God's presence. Years after the event, I met a person who knew Ms. Harriet. She reported that, through the years, Ms. Harriet had developed a secret powerful prayer time that normally lasted five hours per day. The skill of waiting and listening to God is the reason she remained unruffled by the casualness of the teen meeting. As she stood without words spoken, her heart, long trained in God's presence, discerned his will, and from that discernment, she went on to commune with the Father before all assembled. God's presence was her passion, and her prayers were the entry point to him.

In today's church, preparation for leadership is primarily focused on academic education. Will you ponder and pause for a moment? What would the face of the church look like if all leaders were to spend three hours per day in prayer? Should every ministry student be required to pass a "prayer test"? If we practiced prayer as it is outlined here, would we be further along than we are?

I was in my mid teens when I saw Ms. Harriet. I have, after many years, a deep hunger to have what I saw in her. I saw the fruit of a relationship with God not easily won or hurriedly shaped, but once gained, what an impact! There is a wake of that meeting still with me. Visualize it. Altars full of people without asking anyone for a response and caused by three simple words.

Oh God, Less of Us and More of You!

Another dear lady known to me from childhood had a wonderful prayer life. Every Monday she spent eight hours minimum in prayer and waiting in God's presence. Her health became fragile and years of world traveling had taken its toll on her strength. In those years I lived nearby. On one of my visits I asked, "How do you spend your time these days?" The immediate answer was, "I pray." Her pastor had given her a church key and she went there an average of five hours per day. Again and again she said, "I must pray. I must pray more. I love to pray and seek God." Her house was full of the presence of God.

On another visit she had prepared lunch and we were about to eat. She asked me to return thanks and I refused. I wanted to hear her pray again. Immediately she looked heavenward and said, "Father" and off she went into a twenty minute conversation with the Father. The lunch sat and turned cold and neither of us really cared. God was with us. In those moments who cares about food? I was an observer of an encounter of the divine kind.

Something happened very deep inside me that day. With my heart I made a request to God. "Please God, whatever it is that consumes that woman, I want more of it. Show me how to grow a prayer life that rises above request making to communion." *God and I are still working on that request. Would you like to join me?*

Ms. Harriet prayed from three to five hours per day to strengthen her ministry and to grow intimate with God. Her perseverance in prayer caused her voice to be one of great spiritual authority in public service. My second friend used time that most people would call retirement years for the purposes of prayer. Most days she prayed five hours. Many people testified to the great grace that had come to them through the prayers of these ladies. There is a simple reason people were impacted. These women were intimate with God, and out of that close relationship came a multitude of answered prayers.

Chapter Twenty
The Golden Bowls

What is a prayer worth?

There have been a lot of prayers offered up over the ages: prayers over meals, prayers by bedsides, prayers in hospitals. Pilots in cockpits have prayed, civilians in bunkers have prayed, soldiers in foxholes have prayed. Prayers were recited in worship, at weddings and whispered before tests. People have prayed for money, for forgiveness, for love, and for faith. Wives have prayed for husbands, fathers for sons, children for parents. Churches have prayed for crops, for the president and the victims of an earthquake on the far side of the world. Christians have prayed for their unbelieving neighbors and for unbelieving nations, as well as the missionaries who carried the Gospel there. The Holy Spirit has been invited in through prayer and demons cast out. Christians have both cried and fallen asleep during their prayers. Individuals have prayed alone in closets, small groups have gathered to pray together and tens of thousands have gathered in stadiums for a prayer service. People have prayed in their native tongue, in languages they barely knew and in strange languages they have never heard before. Some have seen their prayer answered before they finished it, and some died never getting the answer they hoped for. Prayer has come at the best and worst moments in people's lives. Prayers have reconciled enemies, healed bodies, infuriated torturers, converted prodigals, dedicated cathedrals, encouraged cowards and–in some mysterious way we don't completely understand–bound and loosed heavenly forces. Prayers have been sung to music, murmured in the dark, written into books, broadcast over radio, shouted over ships' decks in a raging storm, and printed in church bulletins. Christians of every nation, tribe, race and language have prayed in every century, in every time zone.

What have all those prayers been worth? Priceless.

The Book of Revelation contains some imagery that is hard for us to grasp. The Apostle John struggled to describe heavenly things in human language. We joke that a new food "tastes like chicken" because we have nothing else to compare it to. How much harder was it for John to describe the throne room of the Ancient of Days? When John grasped for images to describe the indescribable he reached for things that were familiar and significant to his readers in the Roman world of the first century, like lamp stands and candlesticks, which are less meaningful to us in the twenty-first century.

One of those images which impresses us less than it did the people of John's day is a golden censer. First of all, most of us don't know what a censer is (it's a kind of chalice, usually hanging from a chain, that held burning incense in the worship services of the ancient Greek world, and still does in Greek Orthodox churches). Also, we live in an age of greater material wealth, and finely-crafted things are a more common sight today than they were then. Granted, we don't see censers made of solid gold that often, but gold-plated items are fairly common. Moreover, our artistic tastes are quite different than those of the Roman world, and a golden censer might not exactly be our cup of tea, so to speak.

For these reasons (and others) many of us get bored by the descriptions of the golden bowls and censers in the Book of Revelations. That is a mistake. If we slow down and listen to the story that John tells, we will learn what our prayers are worth. More than that, we will discover something so shocking that it will change the way we look at God, history, and our own lives.

John describes all the ornaments and articles of worship in God's throne room as being made of gold. We don't know (yet) whether they actually are gold or some heavenly substance that John can only describe as gold. There are lots of golden bowls, but the first ones we are interested in appear in Revelation chapter 5: "...the four living creatures and the twenty-four elders fell down before the Lamb. Each one had a harp and they were holding golden bowls of incense, which are the prayers of the saints."

Let's back up and set the scene. In Revelation 5 John sees "in the right hand of him who sat on the throne (God the Father) a scroll with writing on both sides and sealed with seven seals." What is the scroll? Bible scholars offer differing opinions, but I believe that the scroll is God the Father's will for his creation. It is his plan for history, and the seals are impenetrable, meaning that no one can read the will of the Father for this world. But there is a problem: not only can no one know the will of the Father, no one can release it and bring it to fruition. Which means not only that the creation cannot receive his perfect justice, but his perfect mercy, wisdom and grace.

Then John sees a mighty angel, who shouts across the vast expanse of heaven, "Who is worthy to break the seals and open the scroll?" We then read one of the saddest passages in the Bible (5:3-4), "But no one in heaven or on earth or under the earth could open the scroll or even look inside it. I wept and wept because no one who was found who was worthy to open the scroll or look inside." In all the universe, no one was noble, good or powerful enough to know the will of the Father and share it with a broken creation, groaning under sin and longing for liberation (Romans 8:21-22). John weeps and weeps because, like prodigal sons languishing in a pig pen in a distant country, we cannot be reconciled with our Father.

Then one of the elders (saints) tells John to stop crying. He exclaims to John (we can almost imagine him grabbing John's shoulder and pointing), "See the Lion of the Tribe of Judah, the Root of David, has triumphed. He is able to open the scroll and its seven seals." John looks and, instead of a lion, sees a lamb "looking as if it had been slain." That probably means that it had blood on its wool and an ugly, sacrificial scar around its neck. This lamb that had been killed and was now alive was standing in the center of the throne (at the right hand of God the Father). The lamb has seven horns and seven eyes, which John tells us are the seven spirits of God sent out into all the earth. The lamb comes and takes the the scroll from the right hand of the Father.

That brings us back to verse 8: "And when he had

taken it, the four living creatures and the twenty-four elders fell down before the Lamb. Each one had a harp and they were holding golden bowls of incense, which are the prayers of the saints."

And so, at this pivotal moment in the story of the universe, *it is the prayers of God's people* that adorn and honor the risen Son as the Father empowers him to bring about the Father's perfect will, justice, wisdom, and grace.

What are our prayers worth? What are *your* prayers worth? Stop and reflect on this: they are a beautiful aroma before the Son as all the authority of the Father is given to him. They rise from golden bowls in the hands of the cloud of witnesses who have gone before us. Our Lord is blessed and praised and given honor by the worship of God's people, and their prayers are the sweetest part of that, rising and covering the whole scene in a beautiful mist.

Most of us who are parents have a drawer or box full of our children's artwork: pictures they drew for us, holiday cards they glued and glittered and signed with X's and O's, little crafts they brought home as gifts from school or camp. If our houses were on fire, most of us would probably grab that box as we ran out. It's precious to us because it is a collection of the affection of those we love and value the most. Our prayers are like that to our Lord. The lamb who was slain willingly bled because he loved us more than his own life. He loved us more than his own status and throne. The prayers of his children, the children he gave it all up for, rise from those bowls and bless him as he is blessed and empowered by his Father. What are your prayers worth? They are priceless.

If we stopped there, that would be quite a lot, but there's more. All those prayers we described at the beginning of this chapter do not just bless the Son as he receives the scroll. They are an integral part of bringing what is written in that scroll to fruition. Our prayers are a critical part of the Father's plan and the Son's mission.

In the next few chapters the seals on the scroll are broken, one by one. The will of God is released onto the world. But "when he opened the seventh seal, there was silence in heaven for about half an hour" (Revelation 8:1). All of the praise, all of the activity of the angelic host and the community of saints, all of the motion of God's will just...stops. Have you ever been in a large crowd for a moment of silence? Perhaps at an athletic event, in a stadium? A hundred thousand people are still and quiet. After thirty seconds it feels strange. After a minute people shift and squirm. All the heavens, with assemblies of "thousands upon thousands" of angels and saints (Hebrews 12) are still and quiet for thirty minutes. What are they waiting for?

They are waiting for God's people to pray.

"And I saw the seven angels who stand before God, and to them were given seven trumpets. Another angel, who had a golden censer, came and stood at the altar. He was given much incense to offer, with the prayers of all the saints, on the golden altar before the throne. The smoke of the incense, together with the prayers of the saints, went up before God from the angel's hand. Then the angel took the censer, filled it with fire from the altar, and hurled it on the earth; and there came peals of thunder, rumblings, flashes of lightning and an earthquake."

Rev 4!! I saw a heavenly portal open before me ...

And said, "<u>Ascend</u> into

This Realm!"

God valued the things said to him P.124

P.115 - 6
We become Attuned to the
world of the kingdom

P.120 investigate the heavenly
side of the prayer equation

P.122 Worship intercession are
Ascension ministries

Both require individuals to exercise their
will positively towards God.

Ascension Anointing

The completion of God's plan depends on God's people praying. The Son does not unleash the Father's perfect justice, wisdom, mercy and grace until the adopted children—that's you and me—join in the family business and help bring it about. Heaven is waiting for us to pray.

What is a prayer worth? It is not only the blessing that empowers our risen Lord, it is the last key to bringing about the Father's plan to restore and rehabilitate the creation.

Christ is the hope of the world, but we are co-heirs of his glory, participants in his mission, ambassadors of his Gospel, as if he were making his appeal through us. We are his hands and feet doing his work, we are living stones being built into a living temple in which his Spirit dwells and blesses the world.

All of this depends on prayer. Heaven is silent. Heaven is waiting and watching. Most of all, heaven is listening. Listening for God's people to pray.

What are our prayers worth? They are priceless.

Conclusion

How important it is to pray and not quit. Through the chapters in this book you have been privy to the prayer lives, and the incredible, highly beneficial results in the lives of people from many parts of the world and from many different contexts of need. The common thread between them was not the depth or kind of need, their particular geographical place on the globe, or their culture. None of those things defined their lives or determined their successes. Prayer did—persistent long term prayer. Some people prayed for a lifetime and some for a few years but they all stayed in prayer until they were answered.

There is potential at the prayer point—potential for a whole new life, more intimacy with Jesus, a wonderful sense of refreshing, creative miracles, and a destiny touched and shaped by a kind and benevolent God. We must, therefore, pray on according to the mind of Christ. "Prayer is the mother and daughter of tears. It is an expiation of sin, a bridge across temptation, a bulwark against affliction. It wipes out conflict, it is the work of angels, and is the nourishment of everything spiritual" (John Climacus c. 579-649).

The more I ponder these truths, the more I know my heart needs to expand and grow in responding to God's call to prayer. I do not yet practice praying at all times but I want to. Do you? I am aggressively in pursuit of God and, through him, a better prayer life. Will you join me?

No so in haste my heart!

Have faith in God and wait;

Although He seems to linger long

He never comes too late.

—Anonymous

Endnotes

[1] Whitney, Donald S. *Spiritual Disciplines for the Christian Life* (Colorado Springs, CO: NavPress, 1991), p. 151.

[2] Ibid. p. 152.

[3] Willard, Dallas. *The Spirit of the Disciplines* (San Francisco: Harper Collins, 1998), p. 167.

[4] Engle, Lou. *Harvest Times Magazine* (Pasadena, CA: Published by Harvest Rock Church, March 1991), p. 1.

[5] Ibid.

About the Author

Dale Van Steenis received his spiritual formation in a large local church in the midwest. Since his family was heavily involved in the life of the church, he moved into leadership at an early age. From his mid-teens he has worked in ministry in music, speaking, missions, and youth pastorates. Pastorates have been served in Texas and California. He led a youth program serving more than 400 churches for five and half years. For the last twenty five years he has been the director of Leadership Strategies International (LSI) which has taken him to more than 100 nations. LSI is a ministry designed to train Third World ministers and church workers. Additionally, LSI assists thousands of people annually through humanitarian assistance programs such as medical assistance, food, water purification projects, and agricultural improvement programs. His humor, world wide experiences, hunger for renewal, and strong academic background combine to bring strength to church leaders worldwide.

Dale and his wife Gloria are parents of four children and reside in Southern California.

You may contact him through his website:
www.leadershipstrategies.org

29989124R00121

Made in the USA
Columbia, SC
24 October 2018